Raising a Self-Starter

Raising a
SELF-STARTER

Over 100 Tips for
Parents and Teachers

ELIZABETH HARTLEY-BREWER

DA CAPO PRESS
A Member of the Perseus Books Group

Cataloging-in-Publication data for this book is available from the Library of Congress.
ISBN 0–306–81315–7

Published by Da Capo Press
A Member of the Perseus Books Group
http://www.dacapopress.com

Da Capo Press books are available at special discounts for bulk purchases in the U.S. by corporations, institutions, and other organizations. For more information, please contact the Special Markets Department at the Perseus Books Group, 11 Cambridge Center, Cambridge, MA 02142, or call (800) 255-1514 or (617) 252-5298, or e-mail specialmarkets@perseusbooks.com.

1 2 3 4 5 6 7 8 9—08 07 06 05 04

For all discouraged children

Do not train boys to learn by force and harshness but lead them by what amuses them so they may better understand the bent of their minds.

—PLATO

Contents

**Part Three
Rediscovering Motivation:
Getting Them Back on Track**

Introduction:
The Great Balancing Act

Being a parent of young children at the beginning of the twenty-first century is hard, and it is not likely to get any easier. Parents are under fire. We have to make ends meet in an increasingly harsh and competitive world; we have to manage a variety of family arrangements and new roles; we have to compromise constantly, juggling our needs, wishes and opportunities with those of our partners and children. And all the while we are held responsible for an ever greater number of personal and social ills. Children's underachievement is just one of these.

The stakes are rising for all of us as competition stiffens for places in sought-after nurseries, schools, colleges and, finally, for jobs. The pressure starts early. Children's future behavior, life-chances, talents and fulfillment are significantly determined, we are told, by us in their early years. Of course we want them to get ahead, so we naturally want to get it right. It is a heavy responsibility for us to bear and an even harder one for us to carry out successfully.

In parallel with underachievement, and at the opposite end of the achievement spectrum, we are seeing a growing band of prodigies—virtuosi violinists aged ten, international swimmers over the hill by the age of sixteen, single-minded tennis starlets, mathematical genii hothoused from age five, budding linguists who are starting preschool. With the right learning techniques, we are told, the sky is the limit for our children. If our child is not displaying notable talent in some area or another by the end of elementary school, we can easily think we have failed in our duty to explore and exploit his potential. Guilt and pressure can become relentless.

The parent of a three-year-old mini gymnast was overheard asking the class coach, after only four weeks of attendance, whether her daughter was any good. "If she's not got any talent, I don't want to waste my time bringing her here," she explained with no thought whatsoever for her child's enjoyment. Ferrying children from one after-school or weekend activity to another in case this is the sphere in which they will reach stardom takes not only time but also a great deal of money. There is a growing social and economic divide between the do-nothing children and the do-everything ones. While many children certainly do underachieve, having few opportunities to discover unexplored talents that can help them grow in confidence and pride, others are in danger of being overextended—managed, monitored and chivvied all day long. Social and educational one-upmanship is in danger of stifling the very creativity and motivation the new opportunities are designed to promote.

For many of us whose children merely plod along somewhere in the middle, it can be hard to know which way to turn. Of course we want our children to develop their talents, but when does encouragement develop into pushiness and secret glory-seeking on our part? When do high expectations and the pursuit of excellence—something all schools are now asked to aim for—lead to burnout? Is our child's lack of enthusiasm for some activity a genuine preference, or a result of low confidence and self-belief that need to be worked on? We are in danger of creating a world in which so much is expected that no one has time to rest, neither parents nor children. If we don't ask ourselves some fundamental questions, this search for fulfillment could create as many problems as it solves.

MOTIVATION

Children are people, not puppets, pigeons or performers. A parent's prime responsibility is to nurture the whole child—and to encourage self-motivation. Parents cannot have influence forever. Nevertheless, our early role is vital. With an eye always on our child's evolving autonomy and his need to believe in and manage himself, from the first day of his life we can help to create a motivational climate and energy for him that models good practice and creates a continuing momentum as we gradually withdraw, leaving him in full control. The same approach also works when a child loses heart and direction. The effective motivator does not rely on "secret plans and clever tricks," to quote Roald Dahl's children's story *The Enormous Crocodile,* but instead works openly to build a child's:

- self-belief
- self-efficacy
- self-direction

Self-belief means you have a clear and positive sense of your "self" and are able to view yourself in a favorable light, in many different ways. Children who lack self-belief are filled with a generalized self-doubt.

Self-efficacy exists when you feel capable because you believe and expect you can carry something out effectively. Children who lack a sense of self-efficacy feel hopeless and incompetent.

Self-direction means being able to work independently on tasks and problems. Children who lack the ability to direct themselves feel helpless and become dependent on others to take them forward.

Parents who demand too much and in the wrong way can do as much harm as those who demand too little. We have to aim for a healthy balance, for our sanity and for our children's long-term success and emotional health. This is not a book for parents who desperately want their child to excel and are looking for some quick fixes. Neither does it provide quick or easy answers for those who have drifted away from their child emotionally, who only realize the consequence of this when any problems with motivation become serious. Certainly, there are ways to help rebuild relationships and regenerate motivation, but they are neither quick nor necessarily easy.

Maintaining a healthy balance is often easier said than done. Sometimes, we are blind to our personal style and the extent of its impact. Sometimes, when the point of balance needs to shift, it takes us a while to recognize this. Outside influences and pressures may become too strong to resist. At other times, we may have neither the emotional nor the financial resources to reflect or give much at all. Nonetheless, if we are able to think a little more deeply about our own motives, goals and tactics; acknowledge and respect our children's feelings and perceptions, dreams and fears; and keep to some fundamental principles of good practice that enshrine the three guiding "self" beacons above, we are more likely to steer a successful middle course.

The middle course is achieved when you show interest, but aren't intrusive; offer direction, but aren't directive; encourage talents, yet leave the child in control; contain, but don't confine; establish routines, but build in flexibility; support and encourage, but don't control and push; offer choices, but avoid being manipulative.

The effective motivator realizes that self-motivation depends on building quality relationships. The effective motivator trusts, respects, listens, encourages responsibility wherever possible, allows choices, nurtures competence and shares the trials and tribulations of effort, success and setback.

The parent who is most likely to have a relaxed and self-motivated child:

- works with, not against, the personality and character of each child;
- starts from where their child is, not where they or others want him to be;
- encourages curiosity;
- ensures experience of success;
- offers the chance to try himself out;
- focuses on the positive;
- values a wide variety of skills;
- helps a child to help himself;
- does not make approval conditional on success;
- does not compete;

- takes no "ownership" of his efforts and achievements;
- provides a stable, predictable and trusting environment.

All these issues are explored and developed later on in the book. It offers practical guidance and wider understanding on the subject of motivation and children. It offers suggestions both to parents who have children going through difficult times and to those wanting to establish a positive motivational environment from the beginning. Although it is not a psychology book, we must understand that words and actions, interpretations and assumptions, make a difference. Emotions and feelings, particularly about ourselves, lie at the heart of learning and striving. Managing motivation is about managing relationships. It is therefore important to understand something about the reasons behind the behaviors we see.

Part One of this book develops our understanding of motivation. It looks at what different people mean when they use the term; develops a model of motivation that sees it as a process and identifies five stages within it; and explores the part played by self-esteem in generating self-motivation.

Part Two presents the principles linked to each of the three beacons. The importance of each one is explained, before exploring how to put it into practice. Wherever relevant, different strategies will be suggested for children of different ages; what works for children at one stage of childhood won't necessarily work at others.

Part Three looks at some common motivational problems and offers suggestions for getting children back on track. It also shows what might lie behind some of the difficulties. Most problems are progressive. If we understand why things might have gone wrong at the "serious" end, we can become more aware of general good practice, which should prevent problems surfacing.

PART ONE

Understanding Motivation: Issues and Ideas

1

What Is Motivation?

Motivation is something most of us feel we don't have enough of. We know it is important; it helps us to feel fulfilled, and it helps us to feel responsible for ourselves and in control. It is fundamental to personal development, contentment and success. Without it, either our potential remains untapped or we end up where chance directs us, not having taken control of our own life. In either case, we can be left with a sense of disappointment, a feeling of "if only . . ." that can eat away at our self-respect.

As parents, if our children do not seem motivated, we worry that they might not do themselves justice, that they might get led astray or even waste their lives. We are certainly likely to feel guilty, wondering whether their lack of purpose has something to do with us, despite finding ready excuses in unsuitable friends, poor teachers, absent partners, television or hormones. On a purely practical level, life is so much less stressful and more pleasurable if our children have it.

Motivation has been likened to fire, a source of energy that sustains commitment. But remember that fire requires fuel. Parents provide some of that fuel, but, as with real fires, too much fuel cuts out the life-giving oxygen and will smother the fire and extinguish it. We must be constantly aware of the difference between child-directed and parent-driven motivation.

If we get the two confused, our interventions can backfire. It helps to understand more about the language of motivation.

Motivation can manifest itself in many ways:

- inspiration
- perspiration
- aspiration
- explanation
- self-exploration

MOTIVATION AS INSPIRATION

For some people, motivation is mainly about energy and enthusiasm, passion and purpose. Inspiration is the key. It expresses something very personal about what someone likes or wants—what makes them who they are. The passion creates both the commitment necessary to stick at tasks when they become difficult and the desire to perform tasks well.

It would be great if all children were inspired. The trouble is, they are often not. Children's lives are full of things they have to do that we cannot expect them to get passionate about. For example, few children exult over homework. It is a rare child who gets excited about keeping his bedroom tidy, or is inspired by every subject that he has to learn in school. There are also times during childhood when things that children had been passionate about lose their appeal and times when personal problems can leave a child feeling empty and directionless. Where passion and inspiration coexist, parents have few problems. The issue, for parents and professionals alike, is not only how to stimulate and impassion children but also how to keep children focused when passion falters or when there is little scope for inspiration.

MOTIVATION AS PERSPIRATION

The common definition of motivation is the degree of effort made to achieve ends or goals. Words like "willpower," "diligence," "perseverance," "fortitude," "tenacity" and "self-discipline" come to mind. Some people in education today think that children have become featherbedded, and have lost the ability to work at things simply because they have to be done, even if they are not enjoyable.

Of course, a measure of self-discipline, or steadfastness, is important to anyone in achieving their aims, whether or not they are fueled by passion. But this understanding of motivation is both limited and potentially dangerous. It is limited because motivation is a subtle and complex process that involves many skills, experiences and understandings, not just fortitude.

MOTIVATION AS ASPIRATION

Motivation also involves aspiration. We have to have goals, targets or objectives to aspire to. Motivation is therefore about having a sense of direction, having ambitions and a clear idea of what we want to achieve. Role models can be very important as examples of what is desirable and possible—of who or what we might like to become or do.

If we aspire to something, we look up to it. It requires a stretch. It might be almost out of our reach, but we have to believe that it is attainable. The language of aspiration includes words of optimism and expectation such as hope, wish and desire.

MOTIVATION AS EXPLANATION

Unlike the first psychologists to study motivation who understood it in terms of inner, almost elemental and uncontrollable, "drives" or "urges" that fulfilled unconscious human needs, people now tend to view motives as rational, and conscious, reasons for doing something. If we understand why we want to do something, we are more likely to work at it. For example, someone's motivation for getting involved in a sport can range from wanting to get fit, through wanting to do better than a brother or sister at something, to wanting to be best.

MOTIVATION AS SELF-EXPLORATION

Motivation is also about the excitement of self-exploration and self-discovery. If we did not feel pleasure in discovering new skills, talents and untapped personal resources, we would be far less inclined to make the necessary effort. Even if we have had to do or withstand something difficult, something that might border on the intolerable such as climbing Mount Everest, we can take pleasure in discovering a new capacity to cope. Once this challenge has been met, we feel safer and stronger. Striving and exploring our capabilities increases our self-knowledge, self-respect and self-confidence.

Self-exploration implies three things:

- discovering what we can do
- undertaking this oneself, on one's own
- initiating the idea, self-generated through curiosity

The achievement is greatest when all three features are present.

The more others intervene and do things for us, the less we can take the credit. Of course, sometimes we need help when we get stuck. And we can usually achieve more if we work as part of a team. Nevertheless, nothing quite matches the thrill of doing something on our own from start to finish: having the idea, implementing it and then completing it.

MOTIVATION AND LEARNING

Given the strong link between motivation, self-development and learning, it is helpful to appreciate two central features of learning. First, learning is risky, as it raises the possibility of failure: we just might not get it right. If we cannot take that risk, we cannot progress. All children make mistakes as they explore and experiment. Through mistakes, they learn what does and does not work, so it is vital that children don't shy away from them. The stronger our sense of self, the more we can cope with setbacks and criticisms. Self-belief comes not from a sense that we are perfect but from the knowledge that we are good enough but have more to give.

Second, learning is potentially threatening as it requires us to change. For children who are secure, this can be exciting. For the vulnerable and uncertain, it can be uncomfortable. If we do not really know who we are, we cling on to an idea, or outer shell, of ourselves. Changing means letting go of that idea, which can be disturbing and frightening. When children do master new information and skills, they have to prove it through answering further questions correctly and taking more tests, and then face yet more. People with low self-esteem have neither the courage to take chances nor the confidence to change. Those who can't meet this challenge will find it easier to stop trying and drop out.

DEFINING SUCCESS

Important though educational achievement is, a parent's task is about far more than helping a child achieve academically. Deep down, we probably all know that neither good test results nor excellence in any sphere automatically guarantees personal happiness or even success in chosen careers. This commonsense view is now supported by research: possessing a range of personal qualities contributes more to success and personal fulfillment than qualifications. At the top of the list is the ability to get along with others. For this, we need to be able to:

- understand other people's perspectives;
- be adaptable;
- communicate effectively;
- defuse potential conflict;
- share decision-making;
- be aware of how we come across to others.

These qualities, widely described now as "emotional intelligence," help people to progress faster and farther than those whose sole claim to fame is impressive paper qualifications. These attributes are also the key components of motivation. If we want our child to be successful, we need to attend to his social and emotional welfare as well as his academic development. In this book, we shall see that many of the attributes mentioned hinge on a positive sense of self, and that this is as crucial to motivation as it is to wider social success, however it is defined. The next chapter explores the link between self-esteem and motivation in more detail.

2

Self-Esteem: The Heart of Motivation

People who feel good about themselves produce good results. To be motivated, a child has to believe he can make the grade. On a more practical level, he also needs to have some idea of how to do it. Someone else's ideas may help, but they will only offer real support if he can make sense of them and put them into practice. He has to, in a sense, "own" them. When in control, he can judge his own progress instead of relying on other people's views and expectations. He can view success and setback as stepping-stones in his unfolding life and not as "proof" of his self-assessment or as unalterable omens of his future.

In early childhood, self-esteem and self-image are shaped by others. The feedback we get from people whom we love, trust and admire has a profound impact on our self-belief and therefore on our motivation. Children feel confident and effective when:

- someone else has let them know that they have done well;
- they have been given responsibility and have carried it out effectively;
- they have been understood, trusted, respected;

- they feel physically and emotionally safe;
- they feel accepted for who they are;
- they are clearly enjoyed.

If, on the other hand, children are punished and ridiculed; if they are reprimanded for trying new things, asking questions or making mistakes; if they are constantly criticized; if they have been ignored and made to feel insignificant; or if their parents' expectations are so high that pressure and failure become unavoidable features of their lives, children will close themselves off, leaving their potential untapped. Parents can help children to become self-motivated by:

- creating some baseline expectations for performance and behavior;
- establishing helpful practices and routines until these are taken on by the child;
- showing interest;
- nurturing a child's self-esteem and self-belief.

Children are more likely to do well, explore their potential and be satisfied with what they have achieved if they have strong self-belief, as well as a sense of self-efficacy and self-direction. These are our three beacons.

SELF-BELIEF

Children with self-belief have a clear and positive sense of who they are. They are able to view themselves in a favorable light, in many different ways. Children will believe in themselves when someone else has demonstrated a belief in them. Those who lack self-belief experience self-doubt.

The Building Blocks

Feeling Understood and Trusted. Children's self-belief takes root when they are trusted, respected and listened to, and when others show faith in their ability to manage things. Self-belief starts with plenty of positive and successful, practical and emotional experiences with people whose opinions, judgments and company they value. Warm, positive, understanding and loving relationships protect children from feeling that there's something wrong with them: they stave off self-doubt and uncertainty.

Knowing Who We Are. Children cannot believe in themselves if they have no idea of what they think, what they like or do not like or what their strengths and weaknesses are. They have to have a clear identity, or self-concept, so parents have to give their child chances to find out about and express themselves.

Knowing We Can Do Things Well. Children get pleasure from knowing they can do things well, but their self-belief will not be strengthened if any particular achievement is considered a fluke. They need to be able to recognize what "well" means. With no sense of how they managed it or what made it good, they have no confidence they can repeat it. Clear targets and detailed and accurate feedback help children to both understand why they were successful and set their own standards.

An Optimistic Attitude to the Future. The fourth building block is a belief that doing well is worthwhile, because the future is viewed optimistically and can be influenced. We are able to hope. If someone says, "There's no hope for you," "You are hopeless!" or "More of this and you'll end up on the scrap heap," hopes will be dashed. The future is cut off, leaving little space for self-belief to flourish.

Strengthening Your Child's Self-Belief

Here are some tips to strengthen your child's self-belief. Try to:

- make it safe to make mistakes;
- help him to know and feel good about himself;
- find something he is good at, and appreciate his skill;

- see things from his point of view, and show respect for his interests;
- give him hope, about what he might be able to learn and do;
- help him to feel safe and optimistic about the future;
- avoid nagging and unconstructive criticism—keep it to a minimum;
- make him feel important and significant to you, through spending time with him and showing interest in his thoughts and what he does.

SELF-EFFICACY

Children have a sense of self-efficacy when they feel capable of managing a number of things effectively, when they believe in their capacity to be successful. Self-efficacy helps them to be confident when faced with a challenge, and to stick at tasks until they master them because they know persistence works for them. Children who lack this belief that they are capable feel hopeless and incompetent and give up easily.

The Building Blocks

Other People Respect Our Skills. Confidence grows through competence. Children pick up our hidden messages. If we assume they will manage, they will feel more confident.

Discovering New Skills. Everyone has a talent and is therefore capable of doing something well and taking personal pride in this. Encouraging a range of talents will help a child to feel competent and effective. There are many everyday skills that help children to look after themselves and fit in well socially, as well as particular talents that help them to achieve more notable success. Families and schools are sometimes rather one-sided in the talents and activities that they encourage and celebrate. Every child is capable of enjoying and doing well in a wide range of hobbies and interests and so should be given plenty of opportunity to do so.

Experiencing Success. Nothing succeeds like success. This is common knowledge, yet we can be remarkably inept at setting the right sort of—or, indeed, any—targets that, when met, generate the pleasure of success. Different children need different targets. High flyers need targets some way ahead; those who are less talented need targets set closer to their current skill level. What is important is not what is achieved in absolute terms, but that it be a significant achievement for that individual.

Developing Responsibility. Giving children responsibility is important. It makes them stop and think beyond the immediate moment. Only through the experience of responsibility can we discover that we are reliable. As Charles Handy has explained, "We need responsibility in order to find out about ourselves." Responsibility gives us the chance to uncover untapped inner resources.

Strengthening Your Child's Sense of Self-Efficacy

Here are some tips for increasing your child's self-efficacy. Try to:

- at every age, encourage him to develop practical, self-help skills;
- let him do things his way and at his own pace;
- find out what he's good at and let him fly!

SELF-DIRECTION

Children who are self-directed are able to manage skills, tasks and problems independently. They have a degree of control over themselves and feel able to influence at least those aspects of their lives that are currently important to them. Children who lack the ability to direct themselves feel helpless and become dependent on others to take them forward. Being able to control, or at least influence, both your present and your future is vital.

The Building Blocks

Being Trusted.   We must know that we can manage our body and our life, and that we are entitled to have a say in what happens to us.

A child's first experience of self-direction, making him feel capable rather than helpless, will be whether his mother or caregiver understands and responds to his basic needs: for food, warmth, comfort and attention. Older children will develop their feelings of "mastery" further if they are given increasing responsibility for managing themselves, are encouraged to question, explore and express negative as well as positive feelings and learn how to negotiate.

Autonomy Through Choices.   Choices are important. We express and define ourselves through choices, because they say something about who we are. Asking a child "Do you want to do this task this way or that way?" not only helps him invest something of himself in the task, but also gives him some control over what he has been asked to do. Used appropriately, choices also reinforce personal responsibility. The very act of making a decision encourages a child to accept an important commitment to the consequences of that decision. However, children should not have free choice about everything. The younger the child, the more we have to manage and limit his choices.

Experience of Independence.   Self-direction and independence feed each other. The more self-directed children are, the better they can manage independence. The more independence they are given, provided it is appropriate, the more they develop the confidence and skills to become self-directed and self-reliant, and show initiative and creativity. The more adults tell children what to do, the less competent they will feel—so they end up asking for direction. It is self-fulfilling: directive parents produce dependent children.

Time Alone.   Children cannot become self-directed if they are monitored and chivvied every minute of the day and have no discretionary time—time that is theirs to fill as they please.

Boredom is not unhealthy. That awful whine, "I'm bored!" can give us a heavy heart, but boredom represents a pain barrier through which children have to pass to help them explore their inner resources and find new interests.

Strengthening Your Child's Self-Direction

Here are some tips for increasing self-direction. Try to:

- encourage independence, within appropriate limits;
- give him practice in making decisions that directly concern him;
- encourage him to take some responsibility for tasks appropriate to his age;
- allow him to spend time on his own, without the television on, which will encourage him to have ideas of things to do;
- let him do things his way; don't force your way on him;
- encourage him to plan ahead and manage his time;
- give him an allowance as soon as he can understand money, so his spending decisions are his.

THE ROLE OF "SELF" IN LEARNING: LISTENING, CONCENTRATION AND MEMORY

Learning involves listening, concentrating and remembering things. None of these processes is as straightforward as it might seem. Children who have problems with learning often find the processes involved difficult. How comfortable we are with ourselves influences how well we listen, concentrate, take in and remember things.

Listening

We begin life as natural listeners. A baby's life depends on communication; he has to listen to sounds as part of learning to talk. As we grow older, however, we listen less and less well. We become increasingly selective about what we want to "hear." Increasingly, we only hear what we want to hear, which tends to be things that reinforce our views and values. In particular, we may avoid listening to things that could imply criticism, could create feelings of failure and that might require us to respond in unwelcome ways. Many people end their life at the other end of the listening spectrum. They become more and more fixed and inflexible and end up as natural "ignorers." But so do some children; those who are hurt frequently or feel threatened by what they hear build the barriers much earlier.

If we start as listening "naturals," why is it so hard to sustain? What goes wrong when people tune out or fail to "hear" what another person is saying? What is it about true listening that is so difficult? It is difficult for several reasons. First, it requires us to let go of ourselves and sometimes to confront the unexpected. Second, it involves empathy and understanding. Third, it sometimes requires action and, occasionally, demands that we do something or change ourselves on hearing the message. Listening is potentially threatening because it can disturb our equilibrium, or status quo, especially if we are feeling vulnerable, so we stop doing it.

When Children Find It Hard to Listen

Children have to listen to hear—things like instructions. They have to listen to learn—things like explanations. They have to listen to remember, recognize and also to understand. A child who finds it hard to listen may have a low concentration threshold because he is maturing at a slower rate and remains very self-focused. He may be bored because he genuinely knows what it is he is being asked to work at. He may be switching off because he has not understood something explained earlier, and the further information cannot be understood, processed or pigeonholed. He may, however, have emotional problems that absorb him, or he may cause a commotion to block them out.

We can encourage our young child's listening skills simply by:

- talking with him as much as possible, providing the conversation is relatively free from criticism, blame, reprimand

and other negative messages that a child will not want to hear;

- reading to him, and talking about what we have read, so he is encouraged to listen in order to understand;

- making eye contact as we talk, which will encourage him to look at us in return and notice our expressions, focusing his attention on nonverbal communication and reinforcing his ability to read body language;

- encouraging singing, especially songs that involve body actions and repeated sections that invite the child's participation, which require him to listen to know when to add his special bit;

- listening to and concentrating on sounds in the garden, park or busy street, to musical sounds and rhythms on the radio, by closing our eyes;

- playing sound guessing games of a "What am I?" kind, in which the child has to interpret the sound of the animal or object being imitated;

- above all, listening to him, so he will learn to listen to you and others in return.

Concentration

Listening requires concentration and to concentrate we need to be relaxed. Normally, we think of relaxation as a physical process involving muscles. Muscles are relaxed when they are floppy and not doing any work. Concentration does not need to involve this type of relaxation, but to concentrate, we usually have to stay quiet physically. Crucially, we also have to release our minds—let go of, or break through, our "self" defenses and go inside ourselves.

When Children Find It Hard to Concentrate

Many things can cause poor concentration in children. It can be dangerous for parents to jump to conclusions about their particular child. Although it is undoubtedly true that we still do not fully understand how the human mind works, there are some patterns. As with listening, personal problems—fears and anxieties—can prevent concentration. Boredom can impair it too. But for some children, the process of letting go is akin to losing themselves and is sufficiently unfamiliar and frightening that they find it almost impossible to do. In extreme cases, this may lead to children never sitting still, never apparently controlling their thoughts and never doing anything unless it is a clearly defined, short-term task with a clear, and therefore safe, outcome.

While some children find it hard to concentrate, the majority of younger children will not understand what concentration means. They either do it or they don't. I clearly remember getting a school report when I was ten in which Miss Parkins complained about my lack of concentration, but I did not have a clue what she meant. When my parents urged me to try harder to do it, I had no idea what I had to change in order to create this desirable state. So beware challenging your child with the question "Why do you find it so hard to concentrate?" If you do, the likelihood is that you will not get a meaningful or a coherent answer.

How can parents help a growing child develop the kind of effective concentration that will help him to think creatively and apply himself well? The best and most natural ways to encourage a child's concentration are through:

- playing
- drawing and painting
- reading
- developing enthusiasms

Later, perhaps he can take up a musical instrument. Playing and reading music encourage excellent concentration and listening habits.

Playing, painting and drawing take a child into his imagination. Play allows a child to express and explore ideas safely—at his own pace. By delving into fantasy, he can forget the present and lose an awareness of time. Imaginative play, especially, helps any child to "let go," to move away from the limiting barriers of reality to discover the rich potential of extended exploration within himself. When a child becomes fascinated and self-absorbed in his own imaginative play, his concentration is both intense and entirely spontaneous.

Reading encourages concentration for similar reasons. When we read to our child, and when our child reads to himself, he can become lost in the world created by the story. "Letting go" to enter that world is safe, either because we are sitting close by or because there is a thread back to reality when the cover closes.

Developing enthusiasms is a wonderful tool. An enthusiasm is like a magnet, drawing a child away from the here and now into another world. A child can be enthusiastic about something conventional, such as fishing or collecting stamps, or about something unexpected. Two young boys I know became obsessed with the mechanics and models of lawn mowers. However strange the enthusiasm is, no child should be teased about it.

Practice at Physical Release

Some children take rests naturally and unconsciously as their mind and body need them. For those who are not so self-attuned or not so able to switch themselves off, we can step in to help. We can:

- encourage them to take quiet time, in a bath, on their bed or in front of the television;
- massage their backs, heads and necks if they get very anxious;
- find out their favorite method of winding down;
- consider introducing certain rituals to trigger the relaxation and concentration process, such as tennis players use before they serve; simply breathing deeply and slowly aids relaxation;
- introduce them to martial arts classes if locally available; martial arts train participants to relax and concentrate, mentally and physically;
- encourage good posture, which helps the lungs to expand well; putting hands on the head with elbows pointing outward while sitting straight automatically puts the spine in

an upright position, which will start good breathing spontaneously and naturally.

Memory

Without memory, we cannot learn, develop or make sense of things. Memory is highly relevant to motivation. If we have difficulty remembering things, or how to do things, we will eventually stop trying. But what is memory? Beyond a certain level, researchers and academics are still debating what it is and how it works. It is easy to see that memory is important for learning and study when it involves knowing and recalling facts, the story line in books, the detail and explanations for scientific processes and so on, which are tested in exams. It is relatively easy to accept the existence of two separate parts to memory—short-term memory, and a deeper longer-term memory, which impacts our understanding and therefore becomes part of ourselves. We can also see that memory is about what information goes in and what is drawn upon to help make sense of this, as well as what comes out.

Memory is not a simple mechanistic procedure governed by logic and rationality; it is locked into, and cannot be separated from, experience, emotion and our sense of self, and it has a similar dynamic. Emotion is central to memory—to both its storage and retrieval modes. It therefore affects learning facts and information, our "procedural memory," as much as it affects our "autobiographical memory," what we remember of our total experience and through which we define ourselves.

When Children Find It Hard to Remember Things

Children who have difficulty learning may not be incapable of understanding. Instead, their emotional state may be preventing them from receiving, holding on to, making sense of or recalling information. A troubled, stressed or vulnerable child will instinctively protect himself by blocking out any knowledge that will require either effort or change. He can fail to listen, fail to absorb the information or fail to remember.

Things are always easier to remember if we can make sense of them when we hear or read them. Completely new information with alien jargon simply goes in one ear and out the other. When we buy our first item of high-tech equipment, such as a computer, we tend to glaze over with incomprehension as the sales person races through the various advantages and disadvantages of different models.

The same is true for children, only more so. Of course, children have to master simple addition, subtraction and multiplication before they can manage calculus. But what is less obvious is that children who are in mental and emotional turmoil will also find it hard to process, therefore remember, any new information. If their lives and relationships contain no reliable pattern, they will not be able to make sense of their world at a fundamental level, let alone more sophisticated information. If they had the right files in their heads, these will have been thrown into disarray by uncertainty, and it will take them longer to locate the right ones to understand anything. The longer the uncertainty persists, the further they will fall behind, being unable to fill their filing cabinet drawers at the same rate as other children, with the result that they make sense of less and less.

Research has shown that, emotional factors apart, the less we use our memory, the worse it gets, and vice versa. We can help our child to have good memory habits. There are several general approaches. Rote learning is one, but only one, approach. Committing facts and figures to memory through repetition can be a useful shortcut to instant recall, and develops a skill, but it is only really helpful if the memorized information is also useful and explained. For example, multiplication tables need to be understood. Understanding ensures information is transferred to long-term memory; and if we can explain and relate events and knowledge in a meaningful way and as part of a wider picture, we will be helping our child to organize and integrate his memories. Explanation is therefore another general approach. Planning and organizing sharpen memory, as does talking about the past and helping children make sense of their experiences. Some age-specific suggestions for putting these generalizations into practice include the following:

Children aged 0–8.

- "What did we do today?" As soon as they can understand, talk about the day's events as a regular bedtime ritual.
- Play games that develop memory skills. For example, play the "pairs" game, in which matching picture or number cards are laid face down and players have to try to turn over an identical pair of cards, remembering their positions as unmatched ones are replaced, face down; and "I went shopping and I bought a . . . ," in which each player is required to add another item to a shopping list of objects after they have recited all the items purchased so far.
- Read favorite books over and over to help children to remember words and stories very naturally.
- Sing simple songs and nursery rhymes regularly to exercise memory.
- "When you were a baby . . ." Tell family stories and events to help make recall safe and fun.

Children aged 8–12.

- Encourage your preteen child to plan his time and organize his environment.
- Suggest that he devise some personal triggers, for example, mantras, to use as reminders, for example, "kit, key, . . . " or take two steps back at the front door to allow time for a final review of what he needs to take with him.
- Use "action" learning—singing, dancing about, marching or any other suitable activity—to help children to memorize their multiplication tables more effectively, or to reinforce facts to be learned.
- Play special audiotapes on car trips to help children learn language vocabulary or times tables.
- Introduce, gradually, other tricks that are useful as memory triggers, such as word associations.

Children aged 12–16.

- Be even more insistent with teenagers about identifying and exploiting their preferred ways to learn and memorize for their studies.

- Encourage them to use sticky notes as prompts, or even their friends via phone texts or calls.

- Avoid conflict because it plays havoc with memory. Arguments churn children up and can interfere with their ability to focus.

- Play fun family games that reinforce memory and recall, such as card games that require players to remember who picked up what, and word games in which each player must name a country, fruit, animal or town that starts with each successive letter of the alphabet.

- DON'T nag and DON'T step in to cover for their forgetfulness.

HUMAN NEEDS

Abraham Maslow, an influential American psychologist who wrote in the 1950s, believed that people are motivated by common human needs. He identified seven different needs, which he prioritized in accordance with his view of their importance to human beings. These needs are now referred to as Maslow's hierarchy of human needs. Those needs, in his order of priority, are survival (food, sex and sleep), security and safety, love, esteem, self-expression, knowledge and understanding.

Maslow developed his approach to help managers motivate people at work, but the basic ideas are also useful to parents. Children have exactly the same range of needs. When each of these needs is met, self-esteem will flourish, as explained below.

The Need for Security and Safety

When children feel safe and secure, they can trust themselves and other people. They feel someone is taking care of them and watching out for their interests, so they feel esteemed and worthy of care. The certainty of their life helps them to predict the future with confidence. They can therefore relax and open themselves to new experiences.

Safety and security are threatened when life seems disorganized and chaotic, when the adults who are responsible for children ignore their needs, perhaps threaten them physically and fail to offer any sense of direction. If this situation persists, children are likely to reject the importance of safety and security as the only tactic left to end their vulnerability. Instead of looking for comfort and security, they may actively court danger, doing things that directly threaten their safety, such as joy-riding, clinging onto trains and other death-defying displays of bravado. It may be seen as fun and it may relieve boredom, but it will also make them feel in control of themselves, and not at the mercy of others. The greater the risks they take, the lower their sense of self-worth. For older children, this risk-taking may give them status within an alternative group, and offer them the immediate comfort of belonging at least somewhere.

The Need to Feel Loved and to Belong

Everyone likes to be loved and to feel important to someone. A child's greatest need is to feel loved and valued by the two people who made him. When he feels loved, he will feel he belongs somewhere. We are underpinned by our sense of belonging, and as children grow, the more groups they feel connected to and can identify with, the clearer and more robust is their sense of self. When they fit in somewhere, it says something about who they are and that there are others like them. Belonging also means that they are wanted, accepted and are likable and acceptable.

When children feel rejected and unlovable, as a result of constant criticism, bullying, cruelty or humiliation, for example, they will erect emotional barriers, withdraw from the painful relationship, and try to demonstrate that they have no need to love and be loved or to belong to that group. They will stop trying to please because it is too distressing to strive for acceptance and not to get it.

They may also feel badly let down and deeply disappointed if their desire for love and attention remains unsatisfied. Eventually, they stop hoping, because it is too dangerous and hurts too much. To escape this pain, children have to assert that they do not belong to those who hurt them or let them down. They will feel unimportant and alone. Unless there is someone else they can attach to, neither their self-esteem nor their self-belief will flourish.

The Need to Develop and Understand

The same negative dynamic can occur with the need for "self-actualization," the need to find out about yourself and develop, and the need to know and understand. A child with very low self-esteem will refuse to learn or try anything new, stating either that he's fine as he is and does not want to learn or that he knows it all already. He may also refuse to participate in tests that would reveal his ignorance. John Holt, in his book *How Children Fail,* writes, "The problem is not to get students to ask what they don't know; the problem is to make them aware of the difference between what they know and what they don't." He has to avoid exposing himself to the unknown or to the knowledge-power of others to avoid feeling even more inadequate, inferior, uncertain and ridiculous.

His fear and self-doubt make him cling tightly to himself, to define himself not by substance and content—a well-rounded view of what is inside him—but by his psychological outline, his frontier, perimeter or "edge." If that outline shifts, is dented or is penetrated, he will be in danger of not only losing his sense of who he is but also feeling frighteningly exposed. This understanding provides a new meaning to the description "edgy." To hold on to this edge, something like a shell, vulnerable children have to maintain themselves in a state of tension. Every challenge threatens penetration. Every new experience may require them to change. Every relationship, particularly a new one, requires them to watch and protect their boundary. They have to remain on constant battle alert.

Yet learning and motivation require the opposite. We have to open ourselves up, trust, believe in ourselves and enter and explore the private world of our inner resources. We have to relax and release our surface tension. We have to let go.

3

The Five Stages of Motivation

Striving to reach a goal is like going on a five-staged journey, which could be represented in the form of a map, because maps show us how to get somewhere. The map is as useful for completing small-scale projects as large ones with distant targets. If children are to get useful support from us, we need to be aware of each of these five stages. We can then respond sensitively and appropriately, as their needs will differ depending on the stage at which they have become stuck.

To pass through each stage, a child needs to have two things: certain understandings and certain skills. Having the understanding without the relevant skill will hamper progress just as much as having the skill without the understanding. The first situation represents the overoptimistic child who does not evaluate his abilities accurately. This is dangerous as it can lead to disappointment and dejection. The second situation represents the underconfident child, who possesses the relevant skill at each stage but does not believe it. The ideal is to have the two enmeshed, for this produces a child who is sufficiently self-aware to judge accurately the effort and skills involved in the task and his ability to deliver.

STAGE ONE: IDENTIFY THE TARGET AND
UNDERSTAND THE REASONS

Although it sounds obvious, it still has to be said that a child has to know what it is he is trying to achieve before he can become motivated. He has to have a target, a goal. Staying with the idea of a journey, the goal is the destination. The more clearly defined the target, the easier it is to keep it in mind and stay on track. It is not very useful to tell someone that they have to travel to, say, New Hampshire or France; he needs to know exactly where in New Hampshire or France, in order to choose a sensible route. It is not very helpful to say to a child that he can have a reward if he is "good" for a whole day, for he has to know what behavior is considered good, and, incidentally, want the approval of the person offering the reward. Similarly, it is not very useful to a child if he says he wants to be "best," for example, at tennis in his coaching group, because "being best" does not tell him what he has to do to achieve that status. His target needs to be more clearly defined.

A target can be selected by a child, or be chosen by someone else or be discussed and agreed upon jointly. Very young children will find it hard to think ahead and make sensible judgments about what is realistic for them, so an adult will have to be involved. However, to be useful as an incentive, the goal must be one that the child is happy to adopt, even if it has been presented to him. He has to "own" it. If it is plucked out of thin air in an apparently arbitrary fashion, it will be harder for him to remain committed to it; it can be dropped again just as easily as it was accepted. The child has to be clear about the reason or reasons why that goal is important or relevant to him. Returning to our journey theme, if we know why we are traveling somewhere, we can pack the right clothes and equipment. Most of us like to know where we are going and why; then we can be more focused and get prepared. It is also important to know when we have to arrive.

Understanding and Skills

The understanding required to pass through stage one can be summarized as: "This is what I want, and I know why."

The skills required in identifying a target relate to self-reflection. Children need to be able to:

- look into the future safely and confidently and see themselves there;
- know themselves well enough that they can identify both what it is they want and what their reasons might be for wanting it;
- select goals that are appropriate, in other words, reachable and sustainable.

Be Confident and Optimistic About the Future. Goals usually take time to reach and are therefore part of the future. To be able to identify and accept goals, children have to be able not only to see that far ahead but also to feel optimistic about the future. The extent of children's time horizons depends on their age; the younger children are, the more they live in the here and now. Their sense of time is undeveloped, and the future is a fuzzy and confusing concept for them. The past, present and future get mixed up, and statements are taken very literally. For example, it is quite common for children starting elementary school to think that they will learn to read on their first day, because they have been told this is what they will do at school.

Once children understand time, they can still have problems selecting goals or taking them seriously. Bad experiences in their past can make them suspicious of the future, as they anticipate further difficulty. It feels dangerous. The more secure and trusting the child—characteristics that tend to emerge from predictable, secure and trustworthy relationships—the more he will be able to look ahead and embrace the future optimistically.

Identify What Is Wanted and Why. For a child to know what he wants to do, he has to have an idea of what sort of a person he is; he needs to know how to describe himself, what he likes and dislikes and what he is good at. He has to have a clear self-concept. A child with a poor self-concept and consequently low self-esteem will tend to go blank when asked about preferences, wishes, strengths and even reasons for wanting or doing something. This may be related to the point just covered—wishing to avoid failure given a general assumption that he is useless at everything—but it also stands alone: if we do not know who we are, we do not know who we can become.

The reasons for wanting to reach a particular target are very important. Reasons are our motives, and the clearer they are, the stronger will be our motivation. Reasons can be honorable or less honorable, positive or negative. Many people make an effort simply to get the reward that has been offered as an incentive. Others may pursue an activity simply because they enjoy it, so pleasure is their goal. Some may take on a challenge to prove that someone who has underestimated and insulted them was wrong or may try to shame or outshine a sibling; adversity can be a strong motivator. Some may strive to succeed to avoid their own children being deprived of things denied to them. It can be dangerous to reject any reason as inappropriate. If we criticize our child's motives, we may undermine his self-belief and infringe the principle that children should be accepted for who they are.

Select Goals That Are Reachable. If goals are to deliver that crucial sense of achievement when they are reached, they must stretch and develop. If there is nothing to feel proud of, if no self-development takes place, reaching the goal will not loop back to increase self-belief or the experience of being capable. Goals that are too easy, then, are not helpful. Goals that are clearly unreachable are a problem too. Self-doubting children sometimes pick impractical targets for themselves in order to jump the gun on responsibility and failure. They stay in control of their own failure, bringing about that which they fear, rather than make themselves vulnerable to someone else's hurtful judgment. By choosing an unreal target, they are also absolved from responsibility for trying. Guiding children in where to place the challenge, if they do not select an appropriate one for themselves, is vital but difficult.

How Parents Can Help

At stage one, we can do the following:

- Try to make home a secure and loving place, to make the future safe.
- Provide a variety of experiences so our child knows what possibilities exist.
- Help our child to define his own clear goals and set clear and manageable time frames.
- Check that our child believes the goals are achievable.
- Ensure that he knows why a target is relevant or important, to him or to us.
- Be specific about the practical consequences of his decision so he knows what to expect—the amount of time involved, for example.
- Encourage reflection on any problems that might lie ahead.
- Check to see whether he has yet considered what he will need to do to meet his target.
- Encourage him to adjust a target that is overambitious, or warn of effort that will be involved. Don't say he won't be able to manage it.

Remember—build their self-belief. Motivation is about exploring our possible selves.

STAGE TWO: ASSESS AND DEVELOP COMPETENCE

Having identified the target, we then begin to assess the practical consequences—determining how we are going to get there.

First, we check to see whether we have the competence— what we need to achieve the goal—having already been aware of our general level of ability when selecting the target at stage one. For this, we need not only to have a certain level of knowledge and skill, but also insight and good self-knowledge, so that our judgment about what we need to learn and can learn in the time frame available is realistic. There is little point in a child deciding to make, say, a toy garage from wood in one week if he has never held a saw, or to make a handmade wool sweater for himself if he has never knitted before.

Second, we need to believe that we are generally capable of success in such tasks. We get this from direct experience of managing something on our own to a successful conclusion, and from being in situations in which we have felt capable and in command. Even very young children can be given opportunities to manage themselves, to help give them this very important sense of mastery. All this contributes to the self-belief and self-knowledge that help us believe we can be effective. But again, this self-belief has to be real. For actual achievement to occur, self-belief has to bear some relation to our ability to reach the target.

Understanding and Skills

The understanding required for completing stage two can be summarized as: "This is what I know, and what I know I can do."

The skills required relate to self-knowledge. Children need to be able to:

- assess accurately whether they have the right knowledge and skills to achieve the target and be realistic about what they may need to develop further;
- have a strong sense of self-belief and an expectation that they will be effective;
- draw on as wide a range of existing practical and other skills as possible.

Assess and Develop Knowledge and Skills. Most challenges that excite us and deliver the best sense of achievement are those that stretch our abilities. We cannot achieve them immediately; we have to develop and extend ourselves. Either we learn more as we work toward the target, so the learning is almost unnoticed, or we need to improve skills before we start. An example of the former is a child who starts to work for a higher placement in a musical instrument audition. Through practicing scales and pieces often enough to reach a higher placement, his technique and skill will inevitably improve. An example of the latter is a child who wants to own a pet rabbit but needs to build a cage for it himself because a new one costs too much. If he has not done more than classroom woodwork before, he will have to practice sawing and hammering on scraps before he starts on the real thing, and he will probably have to go to the library or pet shop to get ideas for a suitable structure first so he is able to practice the relevant techniques.

Have Strong Self-Belief and Expectation of Effectiveness. Having a sense of self-efficacy helps us rise to challenges. If we feel incompetent, we will spend a great deal of time and effort avoiding situations that may reveal our weakness. In other words, the more incompetent we feel, the less we are going to try new things and get better. It is crucial to help children feel generally capable and competent as early as possible.

Draw on a Wide Range of Skills. The more skilled we are at a range of different tasks, the more we can use them to help us acquire even more skills and knowledge. Just as success breeds success, so the more we know and do helps us to learn and do other things more quickly. Children who are physically fit and agile, who can read, who are clever with their hands in making and cutting things, who can reason and mix well with others will have a head start when trying something new.

How Parents Can Help

At stage two, we can do the following:

- Give children plenty of opportunity to do things for themselves so they develop a strong feeling of competence.
- Help to make things happen when they show initiative so they feel effective.
- Introduce them to a variety of hobbies and interests to broaden their skill base.

- Help them to be physically fit and coordinated, so they can feel proud of their body and feel in charge of it, not let down by it.

STAGE THREE: PLANNING THE ROUTE

Having passed through stage two, knowing that you have the raw material to achieve the goal, the next stage is putting together a practical plan of action. You won't be able to build a wooden garage, even if you can saw along a straight line and use a chisel, if you do not have a plan, calculate the measurements and be clear about what has to be done in what order. Planning is crucial. It involves a sense of continuity, looking at the past in order to draw the relevant lessons from it and apply them to the present, and viewing tasks sequentially, step by step. As already stated, children who cannot either look comfortably on their past, or have faith and trust in themselves or in the future, may find it especially difficult to devise forward-looking plans. The more unpredictable and uncomfortable a child's life and relationships, the more difficult it will be for him to integrate his experiences and approach tasks logically, and the more likely he is to be "scatterbrained."

If children are involved in constructing their own plans, they also deepen their commitment to the task, learn more from it and take more responsibility for it.

Understanding and Skills

The understanding required to complete stage three can be summarized as: "This is how to get there, and I know I can."

The child who passes through this stage feels capable and knows he can be effective. The skills required are those that come with self-confidence. Children need:

- planning skills—breaking tasks down into logical steps and stages;
- an appreciation of consequences—if they do this, then that will follow;

- to be able to accept responsibility for completing a task;
- to be able to trust and predict.

Planning Skills.   Planning skills are very useful. Whether it is writing a shopping list or creating a packing list for vacation, thinking ahead about which gardening or decorating jobs it makes sense to do in which order to minimize upheaval or running a bake sale for the local school, planning skills are inevitably involved. Thinking ahead and doing any essential preparation in advance where possible are both part of planning. Without planning skills, it is very hard to see how we can get from A to B. They help to make tasks and challenges manageable. They usually save time, and they also contribute to success. Inspiration may fire us up, but without a detailed, practical plan, our passion can end in tears—the fate of so many new year's resolutions. There is a useful phrase used in management training: if you are failing to plan, you are planning to fail.

Planning skills can be developed in children as they grow and mature. If they are, it will help children to be organized, approach challenges in a systematic way and develop their own routines for common tasks. Good planning skills help children to be focused and self-directed, to become, and remain, self-motivated.

Accepting Consequences.   Some individuals find it very hard to accept that certain things have happened as a consequence of something they have said or done. They don't think about their impact on someone's feelings, about the disruption and work involved in the aftermath of something or about the clearly stated punishment that will follow their forbidden act. They will therefore find it hard to know how to prepare for success, for the same ability to think ahead and predict outcomes is vital if motivation is to become more than a wish or a dream.

Consequences can be appreciated and understood better if they are not just regular, and therefore predictable, but also explained. For example, if someone is not told he has caused an upset following an incident, and why, he cannot begin to appreciate that this could be a consequence. Although very young children cannot think very far ahead, parents can nonetheless pay attention, gently and progressively, to increasing their child's awareness of consequences of both behavior and attitudes.

Developing Personal Responsibility. Those who can see and accept the consequences of their actions are taking personal responsibility for them. They think, "if I do this, then that will happen." They, not somebody else, are the cause of what follows. To be able to imagine what is likely to happen and when, people have to have had consistent experiences, and they must be able to accept that they played a part in the event and acknowledge what they did was wrong, misdirected or unhelpful, so that they can do it differently next time. Being held accountable for actions and behavior is the essence of responsibility.

Being Able to Trust and Predict. It follows from the above that being able to trust and predict outcomes is crucial. If children experience no predictability or consistency, they cannot be certain what the result will be of anything. When there are no guiding patterns linking their behavior to a particular consequence, children cannot take responsibility for it. If children never know, for example, whether parents will ignore, approve or punish them; whether someone will be there when they get home from school; or whether there will be food in the fridge, it will be hard to establish those clear patterns through which they can further interpret their world and feel confident within it.

How Parents Can Help

At stage three, we can do the following:

- Encourage our children to think and plan ahead. To show them how, explain why we are doing things in a certain order. We can explain to young children that the blocks are being put away first because the other toys are stored on top of them in the cupboard. When children are old enough to stay the night with a friend, we can ask if they want help with planning what they might take, before letting them do it on their own. Making models from kits teaches how to approach tasks in an orderly way; and giving older children household chores will help them to think ahead.

- Make our children aware of the consequences of their decisions and actions.

- Let them know how they make you feel—happy or sad. Let them experience relevant "consequences," when they misbehave or flout the rules.

- Give them, gradually and appropriately, the experience of responsibility, first for themselves and then for others. They can be responsible for putting their dirty clothes in the laundry basket, for clearing the table, for packing their school backpack the night before and even preparing a family meal from time to time.

- Chart all changes and behave in trustworthy and predictable ways. Establish household routines and clear expectations about what should happen when. Give children plenty of notice of any change or development that could affect them.

STAGE FOUR: APPLICATION AND DETERMINATION

Those who see motivation as the energy required to reach a goal may see this fourth stage, involving application and determination, as the essence of the process. A well-thought-through plan can prevent good intentions from evaporating, but if the clever plan is not applied or backed up by a determination to carry it out, the result can be equally unsatisfactory.

What helps a child to develop application skills and determination? It is not enough to refer back to stage two and say "self-belief." That is part of the answer, but only part. In addition, if either children or adults are to stay the course, they need to be good time managers, good problem-solvers and logical thinkers to see their way through to the end. And application and determination also require courage and commitment. Courage is needed to try despite the chance of failure and the potential of damage to our self-worth, if not our bodies in the case of some sport-based achievements. Commitment is needed to ensure that we are not deflected by setbacks or easier alternatives.

How can parents help a child to have courage and commitment? Courage grows from receiving plentiful encouragement, being able to live with failure and from previous success. Commitment to a task or target flows from knowing that others are personally committed to you and from having been helped through previous difficulties (itself a form of commitment), and wanting something badly enough.

Understanding and Skills

The understanding required to complete stage four can be summarized as: "This is what I need to do, and I will."

The skills and attributes children need include:

- problem-solving
- self-reliance
- resilience
- time management
- task commitment

Problem-Solving. Staying on task often involves solving unforseen problems when they arise, so planning ahead and anticipating possible problems helps. Even so, there will be times when the unexpected happens. Good problem-solving skills help children to feel confident, self-reliant and self-directed, to manage setbacks and prevent dejection and deflection.

Self-Reliance. Self-reliance is the ability to manage on your own: to know how to think independently, combined with the ability to take risks and to solve problems. Self-reliant children don't need other people's approval before moving forward or doing something new. They also have less need for detailed and constant guidance on how to complete a task. Children who are self-reliant can also be relied upon, and they are more independent, flexible, creative and able to show initiative.

Resilience. If we are resilient, we don't crumble when we confront challenges. We take personal responsibility for errors and don't blame others for what went wrong. Resilient children do not take mistakes or criticisms personally but instead reflect on their practical implications. Life is full of disappointments and difficulties. If we can give our children the self-belief to withstand the knocks and to bounce back, we will have given them something of lifelong value.

Time Management. Life is becoming increasingly stressful for all of us, which means we can feel overwhelmed, reel from one half-done job to another and lose sight of what's really important. Time management skills are vital for getting things done successfully. Identifying priorities and allocating enough time to them, while taking care not to waste time on diversions such as the telephone, computer or TV, help children to reach their goals. When we break down tasks into bite-sized, manageable chunks, do the important things first and take some time out to relax, we work more productively.

Task Commitment. Task commitment, or "stickability," is a very important attribute. Those who can see jobs through receive the positive feedback from their success, which feeds into self-belief. On the other hand, those who readily shirk challenge will generally live with disappointment and failure, which feeds self-hate. The tendency, then, is to retreat into a protective fantasy world, claiming either that an outside factor was to blame or they could have succeeded with greater effort. In this unreal place, the sky can become the limit and goals increasingly unsuitable.

How Parents Can Help

At stage four, we can do the following:

- Encourage our children to believe that they can solve problems on their own. We should avoid stepping in and taking over when they get stuck. Instead, we can support and encourage them and ask "What if . . . ?" and "Might it be possible to . . . ?" questions to help them consider new approaches or directions.

- Act as a model, and involve them when we are trying to solve a practical problem of our own.
- Have the patience to let them do things their way.
- Encourage self-reliance when appropriate.
- Help them to finish tasks or projects if they get stuck and dejected, so they do not get into the habit of leaving things unfinished. This may involve offering them an incentive.
- Give them the strength to stay committed by making clear our commitment to them—by showing interest in things they do at home and at school, by supporting them when they are distressed, and by listening and being there.
- Build their self-esteem and self-belief to increase their resilience.
- Establish routines so children get into good habits of regular music practice, training or work.

STAGE FIVE: SUCCESS

It may seem strange to identify "success" as a stage, albeit the last one, in the motivation process. It is important, though, because we have completed the cycle, and success reinforces motivation. If we don't acknowledge reaching the target, we won't experience the pleasure of achievement that gives us the energy to move forward again when we're ready. Instead, we'll feel dissatisfied, despite the success, because we don't accept the effort and achievement as good enough. This is the predicament of the perfectionist. Where motivation is fired by the desire for self-improvement, as opposed to self-development, there is always room to take the achievement further, to prove that the new, and more acceptable, self is real. When we are not sure, we need the evidence repeated, again and again. This is why perfectionists walk a self-created treadmill.

For achievement genuinely to boost self-esteem, it is also crucial that the success stays with the child and is not "taken" from him by a parent keen to enjoy the kudos.

Understanding and Skills

The understanding required is: "This is what I wanted to do, and I did it."

The skills and attributes children need include:

- being able to praise themselves;
- being able to acknowledge achievement.

Praising Ourselves. "I did well and I am pleased with myself" is a very different statement from "I am wonderful." There is nothing wrong with the first thought. This is not bigheadedness or self-obsession, and it should not be considered socially embarrassing. We all find it easier to acknowledge achievement when others around us do the same. When we can enjoy our own success, however minor, children will be able to follow suit. Praising oneself when, and only when, the credit is due shows self-awareness. But, by the same token, we must also be prepared to be honest about any shortcomings when we have fallen short of the target.

The capacity to praise ourselves relates to self-esteem because we have to feel, as a person, we are worth praising. People who reject praise often reject that they deserve credit.

Acknowledging Achievement. Before we can praise ourselves, we have to know what counts as an achievement. Even small advances can be noteworthy, especially if someone is bowed by self-doubt and did not believe he could do it, if he is in the early stages of learning a new skill or if mental or physical disabilities inevitably limit what he can do. A child's achievements will be easier to accept as praiseworthy if we can focus on his personal progress and compare any performance with the previous one. Comparing him to others could turn a real achievement into an apparent failure.

How Parents Can Help

At stage five, we can do the following:

- Make praise a comfortable thing to say and give in our family. If children are to be able to praise themselves, they have to hear it from others first.

- "I did well today!" Model self-praise by openly showing pleasure at our own achievements.

- Celebrate or mark successes, even small ones, especially if our child feels particularly proud of something they have done or achieved, for example, riding a two-wheeled bike, swimming a width of a pool, cooking their first cake or meal, passing their driving test, winning a sporting or other competition.

- Let our child take and keep the credit for their success, and don't undermine it with sarcasm or any comment that they could have done even better.

- Let him know that it is fine to spend time enjoying his achievement before he takes on any new challenge.

- Let him know that, pleased as we are with his success, we love him for who he is, not for what he has proved he can do.

PART TWO
....

Encouraging Motivation: Principles and Practice

Part Two presents thirteen principles of motivation and suggests ways to implement them. However, as children grow, parents have to adapt. What works at one stage of a child's development will not be suitable or effective at another. In order to remain effective as motivators, parents need to understand their growing child's changing, as well as constant, needs. First, then, is a brief overview of child development.

Children worldwide go through similar phases and stages in a similar order and at similar times. Of course, within this general pattern each child is unique, affected by things like natural talents, opportunities, cultural traditions and family expectations and variations. However, all children need to develop in a well-rounded way: socially, physically, intellectually, creatively and emotionally. They need to be able to make sense of events that touch them, be comfortable with their private thoughts and feelings and manage all forms of learning. Without self-understanding and emotional tranquility, academic progress will be stunted. "Development takes place most naturally," writes Annie Davy in *Playwork*, "when children are accepted, respected and loved—then their sense of identity, confidence and self-worth can blossom."

Children's development can be described in terms of their growing and changing sense of self. Though born with distinct personalities, very young babies have little sense of self. They feel most comfortable when they are intimately engaged with their key caregiver who meets their immediate physical and emotional needs for food, warmth, love and physical closeness. During this first, attachment phase, the significant adults prepare the ground and plant the seed of their infant's self. Around the age of two, children produce the first shoot of a self-conscious and separate identity as they begin to establish and assert themselves. The better prepared the soil, through quality attachments, the stronger the first roots and shoot. Toddlers typically yearn for independence and have an unstoppable urge to explore. This is vitally important, but they also need to be contained by sensitively drawn boundaries, the beginnings of discipline. Discipline is like pruning. That new energy has to be directed to produce a secure, strong person.

The period between three and eight is the Growth of Self. The shoot becomes a full plant. During this time, the main focus is mastery of learning, with the right amount of stimulation but without too much anxiety. It is the peak time for parents to influence attitudes and behavior, the time when children have the chance to flesh out their growing identity with knowledge and skills. Parental presence, guidance and involvement act as a stake to support the child as he grows. Too many negative messages about capability, self-worth or personal traits will stunt the all-important growth of self-belief and produce a weakened stem that will need and seek alternative sources of support.

The period between eight and twelve is the Flowering of Self. All the time, attention and care given by parents hitherto pays off, enabling a healthy, strong, independent plant to hold itself straight as the stake is first loosened, then removed. Parents still need to feed the soil and nip unhelpful side shoots, but radical pruning now will distort the plant's natural form. The flowers represent self-image. When the remaining buds swell and open, the full flowers declare, "Look at me, this is who I am." From this public display of self, through clothes, hairstyles, hobbies, styles of behavior and bedroom decoration, to give some examples, a child is able to express himself and where he thinks he belongs. The earliest forays into self-expression may well be via the safe conformity of fashion. The earlier this happens, the more this is likely to occur. Gradually, peer groups become important to children's identity. Different friends and personal styles may be tried out in the process of testing social acceptability and exploring potential sexual attractiveness.

The teenage years, a time of transition and transformation, see the Redefinition of Self. The plant's energy is focused on the new cycle as the youthful flowers fade, leaving the fruit of the new self to develop and mature. The plant seems less attractive for a time and uncertain of its identity. The parents' role as guide and support becomes important again. As in the toddler years, parents help to strengthen the new self by removing the dead flowers, which teenagers will resent, to prevent premature and multiple fruiting which may weaken the new self. The flowering child is sustained for a time as educational and family obligations are met, but this can go on for only so long. Eventually, nature, through the constraints of the seasons, takes its course, and a full, independent and separate identity is established.

This transformation is most successful and complete when children feel secure and are encouraged to explore and develop themselves safely. Those pressured to fulfill parents' expectations will often reach adulthood empty, confused, dissatisfied and either unmotivated or propelled to search continuously for their true worth and identity. The importance of starting from where children are, not where you want them to be, is addressed in the first chapter of Part Two.

4

Start from Who They Are, Not Who You Want Them to Be

As adults, we are all different. We like different things and have different talents. We think, feel and behave differently. We learn and take in information in different ways. This, what interests us, excites and motivates us, and how we tend to think and respond, makes us who we are, forming our unique personalities. The human brain is astonishing for the great variety it produces.

Children too are individuals. The first principle of motivation is to start with your child: to recognize who he is and his stage of development. Every child is interested in different things and possesses unique qualities. Yet, despite knowing this, even teachers can be surprised to discover that children also have clear learning and working styles, often linked to their personality type. Some children are perfectionist; others are slapdash. Some question everything; others love to be told. Some thrive on routine; others like to wait for the right mood and moment.

Some children are able to remember things instantly having merely been told them; others need pictures to help them understand and hold on to information. Some learn best by reading, having words on paper to digest at their own pace; others are happiest to learn through exploration and trial and error, in a hands-on manner, moving about or "learning by doing."

Children will learn more easily, perform better and be more self-motivated if they can do things in a way that suits them— whether by using sight, sound or touch—and through activities that interest them. Both of my children learned to read at the same age. One launched straight into devouring books and avoided writing for some time, while the other wrote almost compulsively and wasn't interested in reading until later. Children's all-important sense of mastery, their effectiveness and competence, will develop best when they are allowed to start from who, and where, they are.

PERSONALITIES AND LEARNING STYLES

But who are they? It can be hard to know when we are so close. Either we cannot see the wood for the trees, or we see too many things negatively. Human characteristics are like vinyl records, not CDs. They usually have a flip side. Features of our child's personality that drive us mad may be seen as plus points by other people. For example, your friends might see your child as strong-minded, while you see him as argumentative and stubborn. They might see another child as having a strong sense of fairness and great sensitivity to the feelings of others, while you see him as whining and a crybaby.

Having a checklist of characteristics often helps to focus thinking. On page 49 is a sample list to help you build a full picture of your child. Look at the two statements at each end of the scales and mark where you think your child fits.

Add any other important aspects of your child's personality not covered by this list. Instead of seeing any of these features as irritating "faults" that you wish were not there, identify a positive side to each one. Consider whether your child displays this characteristic in every field. For example, a child may have a short concentration span for doing things he is asked to do but can spend longer playing with the family pet or eating food that he enjoys. This will help you both to understand the reason for the tendency and to avoid labeling

On the go all the time						Likes quiet time
Loves to be with others						Likes time alone
Sleep/hunger erratic						Sleep/hunger predictable
Easily distracted						Hates to be interrupted
Vivid imagination						Down to earth, literal
Acts/speaks without thinking						Thinks before acts/ speaks
Short concentration span						Can stick at things for ages
Loves all jokes						Does not quite trust humor
Likes clear expectations						Likes to act spontaneously
Likes precise instructions						Likes to be original
Works at a steady pace						Prefers to work in spurts
Loves facts and detail						Finds detail and facts tedious
Unsettled by changes						Flexible and adaptable
Recoils from new things						Rushes into new things
Likes to be organized						Carefree and disorganized
Puts work before play						Mixes work and play

your child unhelpfully. Try, also, to accept these features as the necessary starting points for getting the best out of your child.

Another way to identify a good starting point for a particular child is to ask yourself what he likes to do and what fires him up. Does he find it easy to sit down and concentrate on games, and if so, does he prefer games involving words, numbers or colors, or games that require moving pieces to get tactical advantage, like chess and many of the fantasy-based board games? How much risk, skill or imagination is involved? Are action games or computer games the favorite, "mucking about" with others or informal ball games. Is he a sports nut or interested in animals? One teacher explained that she got a very disruptive child to make progress academically by acknowledging his passion for gardening and encouraging a classwide respect for his unusual expertise. The answers to these various questions will often be influenced by a child's age and gender. Nonetheless, thinking in this way is useful. It can suggest ways to capture a child's interests, identify strengths and weaknesses to be encouraged or worked on and sharpen our understanding of the unique qualities of our child.

Multiple Skills or "Intelligence"

A third way to become more aware of your child's qualities, or preferred style or starting point, is to consider these qualities as skills. An American educationalist, Howard Gardner, has identified seven different skills that he calls "intelligences." They have equal value in human terms, though schools have traditionally concentrated on the first two on this list because they are needed for academic learning. These seven intelligences are:

- verbal: being comfortable and good with words, liking reading, writing and talking;
- mathematical, logical: being comfortable and good with numbers, likely to get absorbed in counting, ordering, sorting and listing things, problem-solving and thinking logically;
- visual, spatial: enjoying color, pictures and images, liking drawing and art as well as plans and maps;
- musical: sensitive to music, enjoying singing, tapping and moving to music, playing instruments and listening;
- interpersonal: being good with other people, being sensitive to their needs and thoughts, able to share and offer support;
- intrapersonal: being very self-aware, in touch with their own feelings, being clear about their ideas;
- kinesthetic: being physical, includes sporting types—people who like to be on the go, to dance, to climb and clamber—and practical types—those who like to touch and feel, to make or build things with their hands.

Our natural strengths will influence how we best learn. Visual children will learn best through sight and images. Musical children learn best through sound. Physically active children may learn best on the move or through touch. Perhaps some children would find it easier to learn their multiplication tables if they recited them while marching up and down the school playground instead of sitting in the classroom.

These natural strengths are also the starting point for boosting confidence and creating a "motivation momentum." Success in one sphere will flow through to better performance and working and learning habits in another. We can all improve our skills in each sphere through application and well-directed effort if we believe we can do it. Children, especially, need to develop and fulfill their academic potential. But if we are to change, and those new attitudes and skills are to become part of a new "us," we have to start from a place that allows us to understand and identify with the new development. A learning program known as "accelerated learning" uses this approach. It starts from something that a child is good at and interested in. The program has an impressive track record. It has been shown to pay dividends, academically and socially, for children from a wide range of backgrounds.

It is easy but dangerous to try to move children forward by starting with what we like now or liked as a child, not with what they like. You know the sort of thing: "I loved doing such and such as a lad. Why don't you try it?" or "I used to spend hours on my own, playing games against an imaginary friend. Why do you need to have someone around all the time?" Or we can be tempted to say the opposite: "I was quite happy as a kid mucking about with your aunt at home. We were good friends. How come you can't bear to stay in?" The adult's frustration is as clear as the implied criticism of the child. If the suggestion is very wide of the mark, a child can feel insulted that he has been so misread as well as criticized. It is akin to not remembering the one thing that a child refuses to eat and piling it on the plate.

If this sounds clumsy, it is even worse to start from who you want them to be. Comments such as: "Why don't you go and find yourself a Saturday job instead of hanging around the house all day?" or "It would be nice if you could play in the school orchestra. Why don't you try the violin again?" or "Why don't you take up ice skating? I saw a great program about the glamorous life the young stars have" all belie a dream and can undermine a child, again suggesting there is something wrong with the child as he is.

Unconditional Acceptance

Starting from who and where our child is validates him. It is also a way of demonstrating in practical terms that all-important unconditional acceptance, which frees a child up to learn and develop in his own way, true to himself. Once we accept him as he is, he in turn recognizes who he is. The more we want him to be someone else, assume he can be different and ignore his preferred starting points, the more he is likely to lose touch with himself. As we shall see later on in Part Two, we have to accept our children unconditionally if success and failure are to be managed in a way that benefits them in the long term.

Starting with who they are and accepting them unconditionally does not, however, mean there is no possibility of change. It does not mean we lock them into roles and forever see them as strong on this and weak at that. Children often need to change and develop new skills as they mature. For example, a child who is so disorganized that he either gets behind or is reprimanded so much as to lose heart clearly needs to change his ways. It does mean that if we want to help him to move forward, it is best done from a point he recognizes, in a way he can manage and for a reason he can accept. In the words of Gerard Nierenberg, an American writer on management: "People do not resist change. They resist being changed."

START FROM WHERE THEY ARE

The very day I passed my driving test, my jubilant boyfriend took me out in his car to celebrate my newly acquired freedom of the road. It was a specialist mini—a demon-fast job. He was very proud of his driving skills—and was a typical boy racer.

He wanted to teach me how to take the "correct" line through curves to maximize speed and road holding. We left the city and he encouraged me to accelerate. I did not feel comfortable, but I was impressionable. So I tried, took the "correct," that is, straight, line through the curve and only just missed a head-on collision with an oncoming car. It taught me a lesson I shall never forget. Moving children forward too far and too fast can cause them to crash because they are not usually in control. Chapters 12 and 13 discuss the part children can play in moving themselves forward to ensure they feel comfortable with their rate of progress.

BROTHERS AND SISTERS: DON'T COMPARE

For some children, living in the shadow of a sibling affects them their whole life. Insensitive comments from teachers as well as parents, such as "Your sister would not have produced work like this" or "You don't have the same sporting talent as your brother," can ruin pride and kill ambition. I have heard people say that they spent the whole of their childhood thinking they were no good because they were told such things. Someone who has since won international praise for her work in medical research still harbors a grudge against her mother, who used to describe her sister as "the academic one" while she was merely "practical." She felt not only damned with faint praise but also stupid in comparison, when, clearly, she was not.

On the other hand, I heard someone complain that her parents always gave her books for Christmas and birthdays, whereas her brothers were given fun toys, because she was considered the brainy one in the family. She resented this labeling so much that she opted out of academic work for many years, going back to it as a teacher only later in life.

Brothers and sisters of budding athletes or musical stars often feel very left out when parents focus not only attention but also considerable sums of money to foster the special talent of one particular child. The twin brothers of Sharron Davies, the former Olympic swimmer, said they felt they grew up without a father; for several years their father lived abroad with

Sharron while she trained. Even when he was at home, they felt ignored because he concentrated his attention on Sharron. In another case, the parents of a rising ice-skating star sold their house and moved the family into a trailer to finance coaching and competition expenses, and then the starlet decided to quit. It must have been quite a sacrifice for her siblings.

Even apportioning equal praise can be limiting. Saying, "He's the artist in the family, while she's the musical one," may give each child something to be proud of, but will make it less likely that either will explore their potential to enjoy the other's field of interest. If someone feels defined by, and loved and accepted for, a particular skill rather than for himself, it will become something he has to reinforce and defend against intrusion by a sibling. When skills become territories, children can become tribal. If, instead, we make it clear that there is room for more than one artist, poet, pianist or tennis player in the family, and that each child has his own unique ideas, feelings and experiences to contribute to the activity, each one will feel free to explore and develop in every possible way.

The better we feel about ourselves, the more we will explore and discover, and feel enriched and fulfilled. How to help children to feel good about themselves, deep down, is the subject of the next chapter.

5

Help Them to Feel Good About Themselves

Children with good self-esteem feel good about themselves, and "People who feel good about themselves," as the *One Minute Manager* tells us, "produce good results." They are better at making and keeping friends, because they are less defensive, less aggressive, feel likeable and are happy to compromise and give time and attention to others. They are better at playing, because they know what they like to do and feel safe about exploring ideas and places. They are better at working, because they are curious, can concentrate better, are able to take risks and are happy to try their hand at new things. It feels great to do well. Being confident in each of these ways helps to reinforce self-esteem still further. Success breeds success. The more confident we feel, the harder we can try and the more we can risk, so we can get even better, and the benefits spread. It is important to work at it.

If our child is feeling strong and doing well, then we have obviously got something right. We can feel pleased, and we should step back, letting him get on with his life, watching from a distance. For children going through a bad patch, when confidence is thin and discouragement close at hand, what can we do to replenish those inner reserves and help them to restart? We can:

- make them feel loved and wanted;
- give them experience of success;
- avoid blame and unhelpful criticism;
- offer a framework of positive discipline.

MAKE THEM FEEL LOVED AND WANTED

All children start off adoring their parents. They need to believe in the people who brought them into the world and on whom they rely so totally. In return, they need to feel loved, respected, trusted and wanted. If they do not experience this, they will feel very separate at a time they need to feel part of something so important to them. Children who feel unimportant and insignificant to their parents become socially and emotionally isolated and are less able to develop themselves to the full.

We can help children to feel loved and wanted by:

- keeping them safe and being sensitive to their anxieties;
- enjoying their company;
- valuing their ideas, skills and opinions;
- spending time with them, talking, walking, playing and having fun together;
- showing interest in the things that are important to them;
- noticing when they do something well;
- keeping them informed about things that affect them;
- trusting them, their way of doing things and their ability to achieve things;
- respecting their needs and rights;
- giving them appropriate choices, so they can learn more about their preferences, find out what is important to them and have some say over what happens to them.

And the most important of these is time. Survey after survey is showing that children like to have their parents around, even if they are not actively doing anything with them. They like to see fathers as much as mothers. In Britain, men work longer hours than in any other country in the European Union. This means that they spend less time at home with their families. Although young children obviously need more direct, physical care from parents or other caregivers, older children need their parents' time, love and attention too. In research presented at a recent Council of Europe ministerial conference on adolescents and their families, even teenagers reported a desire to see more of their parents. When parents do not, or are not able to, spend much time at home, it seems to have consequences. Teachers have reported a fall in children's resilience in the face of learning blocks or other difficulties. In separate research, by Michael Rutter, children's resilience has been shown to hinge on three factors: a positive disposition (self-esteem, sociability and autonomy), a supportive family and social support systems. Communities and families—and fathers—matter. Children feel good about themselves if they feel significant to the important people in their life. If we are not there, sometimes regardless of the reason, it can be hard to persuade a child that he is significant and cared about. Both his self-esteem and sense of direction will suffer.

Cheering Them Up with Presents

Giving children everything they ask for does not automatically make them feel good deep down. What children ask for is not the same as what they really want. Children need and want security, love, attention, to be listened to and understood and to feel that someone is committed to them. If they believe they have this, they feel accepted and acceptable, valued and valuable, significant and safe and worth caring for. They will have the confidence to present themselves as they are to others in their world. If they do not feel they have this essential love and support, they can learn to ask for toys and presents that seem to represent love and attention. If we are not careful, these gifts can become payoffs to end the nagging or fleeting tokens of esteem rather than the real thing. Presents are no substitute for presence.

Find something they are good at. We should not ask if there is something our child is good at. Instead, we should ask what he is good at. Every child has something he does well. It may be dancing, football, drawing, constructing models, climbing trees, knowledge of insects or animals, skateboarding, rollerblading, swimming or bicycle tricks. It may not be an activity-based skill. He may be good at thinking problems through, planning ahead or getting himself organized. He may understand quickly how people feel and have friends turn to him, be generous or good at choosing presents for people because he senses what others like. He may be a natural leader or able to sort out disputes. He may be good at languages, math, science, history, English, environmental studies, computers, electronics or technology. All these subjects count. He may be dependable, reliable, kind, imaginative or have a strong sense of humor. It would be wonderful to have creativity, wit and humor more valued in schools because they are a lifeline to us later.

The list of different personality features and "intelligences" in the previous chapter will help to identify other strengths if you need further ideas. And if you are finding it hard to identify any redeeming features in your child, try to involve somebody else who knows him well because they will almost certainly see things differently.

Help Them Work Out What's Going Wrong

We can interpret successful progress in many ways. Success should not be measured simply by outcomes or results, comparing ourselves with others. It should also include our ability to manage the process of getting better. We can get a sense of achievement from having mastered a new way of doing something. The first time it "clicks," we may not do brilliantly. Nevertheless, knowing that our progress is in our hands through our own effort and feeling confident and in control are highly motivating. Mastering the skill, or being able to respond constructively to our mistakes, is a milestone to be celebrated. A child needs to be able to work out solutions to problems. "I didn't do brilliantly but at least I now know what I was doing wrong" is as worth applauding as a good result.

Focus on the Positive

Tiger Woods, the international golfer, described his route to the top. He was launched by his father, an accomplished golfer himself. His father's method was to put the ball right next to the hole and invite his son to hit it in. Of course, the son managed it because it was so close. Gradually, his father moved the ball farther and farther away. If he missed a shot, the ball was moved closer again. The father's technique was to build confidence through the experience of success, focusing on the positive achievements, not on failures. In this case, it certainly worked.

Self-Development Versus Self-Improvement

Children who have the chance to discover new skills and talents as they grow are very lucky. They learn more about themselves, and the experience sets a pattern of self-discovery that will enrich the rest of their life. But it can be dangerous. It can go wrong when parents and children see the activity as "improving," making the child better and more clever than not only others but also his former self. This implies that how he was before was not "right." He then has to go on getting better, improving himself, making himself more acceptable, trying one new thing after another. Learning should be seen as a process of self-development and self-discovery rather than self-improvement to make oneself more acceptable.

AVOID BLAME AND UNHELPFUL CRITICISM

If we are to encourage children's self-belief and help them feel good about themselves, we have to learn to cut back on destructive criticism as well as focus on the positive.

In a survey undertaken for a major children's charity, 1,000 children aged between eight and fifteen were asked about how they were treated at home. Just over one in four said they were "often" criticized or reprimanded, but the numbers were higher in larger families where parents had remarried or found new live-in partners and where parents had lower-paying jobs. Clearly, therefore, the situation worsens for children the more their parents struggle with stress. What is not so obvious or understood is the deep impact of criticism on children. The survey asked them about this. Those who said they were criticized a lot (and about half the children were interviewed with their parents present, so we should assume underreporting) reported being cuddled, hugged or kissed and praised less, and spanked, slapped or shouted at far more than the other children in the survey. More than one in three in the high-criticism group said they would be less strict with their own children, compared with under one in four among the others.

How deep the hurt goes is shown in other answers too. The criticized children were far more likely to be anxious—about things like bullying, falling ill or even having their home burgled—and far more likely to describe themselves in negative terms. Criticism, together with insult, shouting and other forms of punishment, clearly sends negative messages to children about how likeable and competent they are, with predictable and damaging consequences for their wider emotional stability as well as their self-esteem and motivation. For too long, we have lived with the idea that only sticks and stones hurt. Words, we were told, are harmless. It is time to nail this lie.

We can appreciate that hurtful things said to our children in the playground will wound, and the damage done by verbal bullying is now better understood. It is far harder to imagine and accept the impact of our own harsh words. We can bully with words too. It is emotional bullying. Constant carping and criticism will make a child feel he can never please and convince him that there must be something wrong with him. Endless chiding and nagging will also make him lose confidence in his ability to think independently, do things his way and develop his own judgments. Constant criticism therefore saps independence, initiative and morale. Whenever he does something, he will be looking over his shoulder, hearing our voice in his mind, wondering what we will say next, and when, and which of his actions or comments will be next in line for our disapproval. Shouting, unwarranted blame and harsh, erratic punishment have a similar effect. They tell a child he is wrong and we are right. They challenge, and in extreme cases deny, love and acceptance. They generate uncertainty; there is neither pattern nor predictability associated with the wounding, which explains the more general anxiety felt by high-criticism children recorded in the survey findings. Power lies with the perpetrator. All children thrive on the approval and acceptance of the two people who brought them into the world. If they fail to please, they feel that they disappoint. A child who lives with criticism, sarcasm, insults, blame and punishment cannot avoid feeling guilty for the disappointment he obviously causes his parents. In such an environment, it is hard for any child to have and to hold onto self-belief, self-efficacy or self-direction, or to become a self-starter.

If we have any inkling that this is what we do, we will want to brush it off with excuses. Initially, at the time, we will think our child has deserved the comment, which excuses our negative reactions; we also consider that we love him underneath, feel certain he knows this and that this is what counts in the end. We might even notice his churlish and defensive reactions and think, therefore, the barbs did not penetrate—not realizing that the shield he has put up is a protective fiction. Also, the more we criticize, the more we believe our child is used to it, accepts that we're like that, so is tolerant of our ways. Sometimes we interpret any anger and hostility he shows to us as a personal attack and a sign that we are rejected, so why should we go out of our way to be pleasant to him? Or, if we sense he is hurt, men, especially, are inclined to believe it's time a child was toughened up with more of the same. But children who "cannot take" even constructive criticism have, in fact, taken a bucketful of it. They are saturated with it, and can take no more if they are to have any energy left to protect their self-respect.

If, or more likely when, we get into these critical phases—for I suspect it happens, at least temporarily, to many parents—it says far more about what is going on inside us than about what our child is doing. If we are of a mind to, there are always things we can complain about in anyone's behavior. To do so means that we are watching and judging, which means we are also controlling and untrusting. Either we expect mistakes, so we make sure we are ready to police the errors, or we somehow need to be judgmental—to feel "in charge" when, deep down, we feel uncertain and directionless. Blame, anger, criticism and punishment help us to point the finger elsewhere, away from us, when we feel under pressure. But all of them undermine a child and will damage his motivation either to do well for himself or to please anyone else.

POSITIVE DISCIPLINE AND SELF-MOTIVATION

Research shows that criticism and conflict feature less in families that practice positive discipline. Some children need discipline to feel good about themselves. This may seem an unlikely statement but, by discipline, I do not mean unquestioning obedience and harsh punishment. I mean having clear guidelines and expectations for behavior, defined limits to what is acceptable, a structure to the day and week and learning to compromise with others. Children gain from the structure and security that it provides, the approving comments when they get it right and the care and attention that supervision implies.

In its original sense, discipline has little to do with punishment. Its roots lie in the word "disciple." Teaching, learning, training and education are all included in many dictionary definitions. In this sense, discipline is wholly positive. It is also a social skill. It is about making sure children have the right skills to thrive and survive in today's world; helping children to manage and control their behavior; restricting and prohibiting certain things not to deprive children but to keep them safe and to teach them to think of others; creating a sense of pattern and rhythm that helps children to feel secure.

It is also practical and useful, and necessary for healthy social and emotional development. Positive discipline helps children to fit in. It creates consistency, predictability, trust and respect. It uses positive demands—telling children what to do instead of concentrating on the don'ts. It is one way in which parents can show their care and commitment. Discipline is not about wielding absolute power or commanding obedience like a dictator. The target should be discipline without dictatorship—based, instead, on fairness and mutual respect.

Positive discipline means:

- accepting discipline as a positive process necessary for social and emotional growth;
- giving positive demands—and making our expectations clear;
- focusing on children's positive behavior—noticing and rewarding children when they have done something right, instead of criticizing and punishing them for their mistakes;
- behaving positively as the adult, modeling appropriate behavior and offering praise, support and encouragement.

Positive Discipline and Self-Esteem

If children are to develop self-esteem, they need to be respected and to feel secure. Firm but flexible boundaries help us to acknowledge and respect our child's needs and feelings while asking for the same respect in return. Positive discipline therefore promotes mutual understanding and empathy, a key strand of emotional intelligence. It also promotes learning. Children who feel secure in their relationships learn to trust themselves and others enough to open up and develop themselves. Harsh and erratic punishment makes them cower, and a permissive approach only confuses, especially when it is interrupted by shafts of cruelty. If we give in, say yes, let children take the lead and offer a different answer each time, we do not give children a clear view of themselves or a predictable environment. More important, it gives no experience of learning to fit in and work with others—another vital part of emotional intelligence.

Positive Discipline and Self-Discipline: The Links

We bring our children up knowing that one day we must step back. We don't have influence forever. At some point, children become wholly responsible for themselves and their behavior. We like to think they will manage their lives happily, cooperatively and productively. For that, they need a measure of self-discipline and self-restraint. Looking at what is happening in society, we are beginning to realize that self-discipline is far harder to establish if we have not had good relationships and helpful support and guidance early on. Positive discipline is the best foundation for self-discipline. Why?

For self-discipline, we need to be able to see a job through, aided by helpful habits and routines. We need to be able to put off short-term pleasure to reach longer-term goals: to put the waiting back into wanting. We need a personal code of behavior, to be able to accept responsibility for the consequences of decisions that affect people beyond ourselves.

If early discipline is going to help, it will contain a child but not confine him. There has to be room for creativity and self-discovery and decision-making. There will be routines, but they won't dominate. There will be freedom, but within clearly stated limits. There will be clear consequences for unacceptable behavior, to reinforce responsibility and to encourage forward thinking about how other people are affected, but not harsh punishment. Through support and encouragement, a child will learn how to stick at difficult things and how to survive short-term disappointment.

The Link Between Self-Discipline and Self-Motivation

Self-discipline sounds very much like self-motivation. They both involve planning and thinking about why things might, or did, go wrong. Both involve willpower. But self-discipline is only part of self-motivation. It is like the filling in a sandwich, with self-motivation being the two slices of bread. One slice is the goal, because motivation involves purpose. The other slice is our courage, our decision to have a try.

To achieve anything, even learning to live within rules and limits, children need support and encouragement along the way.

6

Support and Encourage, Don't Control or Push

Children need our support and encouragement, but it can be hard to know when it spills over into creating false hopes or pushiness. Offer no support and encouragement and a child may have no incentive to try hard. Start to control and push, however, and our efforts may well backfire, with a resentful and exhausted child deciding to snub parents exactly where it hurts—by opting out of success.

GIVING THEM HEART

How can we know whether we are showing interest or being intrusive, whether we are being pushy or a pushover? We will judge this better if we think first about the meaning of the terms "support" and "encourage."

"Support" means to take the weight of something, or take the weight off someone. In other words, like a supporting column of a building or a walking stick, it means sharing the strain or burden.

"Encourage" means to give someone courage—the courage to try new things that, because they are new, lead into uncharted territory and may expose shortcomings. To learn, children need to feel brave. I was reminded by an educational therapist, Gerda Hanko, that "courage" itself comes from the French word for heart, *coeur*. To encourage, therefore, means to give someone heart, to reinforce his self-belief.

"Support" and "encourage" are both enabling terms. This is their essence. Parents who support and encourage help their children to help themselves.

Parents who control and push are doing something very different. Both control and pressure imply more direct involvement—even the exercise of power. They convey to a child:

- that he cannot be trusted to do something himself;
- that he is not really acceptable as he is;
- that in some way or other he falls short;
- that he should be different, and in the way his parent would like him to be.

The expectations and targets set, often designed to flatter and benefit the parent, will add burdens to the child, not relieve him of them. They will tend to sow the seeds of self-doubt, undermine his self-belief, and sap his courage, not top it up. They are more likely to discourage and dishearten, making it harder for a child to motivate himself.

Parents who support well:

show interest	• watch their child doing his favorite activity
	• try to provide necessary equipment—pencils, sports items
	• attend school meetings and events
	• ask about the results of particular things that the child has put effort into
offer help	• take their child where he needs to go
	• are available to discuss a problem

	• suggest planning and time-management solutions
	• try to answer questions
	• clarify, in discussion with them, goals and guidelines
listen	• to accounts of problems or successes
	• when a child feels discouraged
	• to anything he wants to tell them about his life
understand	• the child's own learning style and concentration patterns
make decisions	• when the child is unwilling, unable or too young to make them himself

Parents who encourage well:

show enthusiasm	• celebrate with the child when there's a success to share
	• share his excitement about his goals and dreams
	• don't knock what it is a child enjoys doing
show trust	• help a child to set his own, realistic targets—in a time frame he can manage
show faith	• believe in a child's capabilities and potential to achieve
	• offer him chances to manage things on his own
	• give a child hope and the courage to try
mark achievements	• offer praise and rewards
value many skills	• to ensure each child has experience of success

WHEN PUSH COMES TO SHOVE

Controlling and pushy parents tend to:

- finish tasks for their child because they are too slow;
- manage their child's time very closely with busy, inflexible routines, making lists for them of things they have to do;
- hover over children while they do things, implying they'll need help or correction;
- get physically involved in homework; in effect, taking it over—erasing mistakes, coloring in, redrawing lines with a ruler, unpacking school bags in preparation;
- give corrective advice very promptly, without either asking first if it is wanted or bothering to find out the precise nature of the difficulty, so it is often misplaced;
- be judgmental and critical, sometimes excessively so, even where there is a teacher or trainer monitoring progress;
- point out mistakes immediately, without letting a child notice his error in his own time;
- sometimes be competitive;
- set a new goal as soon as the current one has been reached;
- see any carelessness as a sign of future failure: "You'll never become a doctor if you don't . . . ";
- demand high performance, and punish—sometimes with emotional withdrawal—if a child falls short;
- find a child acceptable when he does well, but not on any other basis;
- talk frequently to other people about their child's latest successes;
- tend to want the child to succeed to feed their own pleasure, not for the child's benefit.

We can help children through a sticky patch when their interest or commitment wears thin, to get them "over the hump." We can make sure they are in a position to do themselves justice when they are competing against others and it matters. But then we should back off and put our child back in control. There are two rules of power that apply in relation to children. First, "The more you use it, the more you lose it" and second, "You bring about that which you fear."

The more parents get involved because they fear their children may not make the grade—make the first team, get top marks on their tests or perform with distinction in musical competitions—the more their offspring are likely to choose precisely that area in which to demonstrate their rebellion and independence. A prime example of this is someone who was threatened with punishments by his parents for anything short of an A and for failure to get into Oxford or Cambridge University. He complied all the way until he graduated, when he chose to work on an assembly line in a factory just to spite them. If we shove someone too hard, he might fall over.

INTEREST, NOT INTRUSION OR INQUISITION

We often show interest through asking questions. How was it? Did you enjoy it? Was so and so there too? How hard was it? If we question the wrong things in the wrong way and for the wrong reasons, instead of appearing interested, we can come across either as spies from an enemy camp or as red-robed representatives of the Spanish Inquisition. Not surprisingly, children will then clam up.

Of course, how our questions are received depends in large part on a child's mood at that moment. Even with the best of intentions, we can end up with our heads bitten off. Teenagers are the most fearsomely protective of their long-awaited and often hard-won freedoms, but younger children have their pride too. These realities apart, the fault can also lie with us. Where we have a hidden agenda for our questions, even young children usually detect it. We have to tread carefully.

Before you fire away, it is sensible to ask yourself a few questions first.

| Why are you asking it? | Is your question straightforward, or are you collecting information to discover something else? Even |

worse, do you already know the answer, and the question is a tactic to trip them up or raise an issue? For example, asking "When is your first exam?" when you know it is next week, is a way to suggest that they do more studying. Better to be honest: "Your exams start next week. Do you think you are ready for them?"

How should you ask it?

The more questions you ask in a row, the more it sounds like a courtroom interrogation with your child on the stand.

Where should you ask it?

Wherever it seems natural, but personal questions are best asked when others will not overhear, and challenging questions should be raised in neutral space, not in the children's bedrooms.

When should you ask it?

When there is time for a considered answer and discussion. Not when they are just going out of the house or have just come in and want to relax. After an exam, for example, children like to be given time to tell you when they are ready. We can say, "How was it, or do you want to tell me later?"

LEISURE IS FOR PLEASURE

More and more children are going to classes, clubs and lessons after school and on weekends. French, math tutoring, ballet, martial arts, various sports such as swimming, soccer, tennis and gymnastics, musical instrument lessons, religious classes and youth clubs are just some of the activities that fill children's "free" time. Some children are so committed that they have no free time left. They do something almost every day.

Many parents fear empty time. In our increasingly pressured society, it is easy to see "down" time as empty time. We worry our child will "waste" time watching television, lazing about, not "developing" himself. We also worry we may be badgered for companionship if he has nothing specific to do. We tend to make sure our child is fully occupied, when many children would prefer to do nothing very much at all after a tiring day or week at school.

How can we get the balance right between giving our children the opportunity to try themselves out, discover new skills and get really good at something, without pushing them to become something they might not want to be? A little shove can be in the best interests of a child. One success story is a mother who let her two boys say no to a range of activities offered until she saw that television was taking over Saturdays. She felt neither had a specific skill he could feel proud of. She enrolled them both in swimming classes, and dragged them along, protesting. As they improved, their protests weakened. When each one started at a new school with swimming available on-site, the Saturday lessons stopped. Each child was then selected for the school swimming team, which delighted them both. Similarly, there are many professional musicians who credit their parents for making them stick to it during the difficult times. However, it does not always work out like this. One mother of two young girls under seven who took them to various after-school activities against their will was becoming depressed by the constant arguments. After attending a parents' discussion group on the importance of play, she changed her mind and stopped every activity. She reported that home life was now significantly more peaceful and everyone was happier.

Leisure is normally understood as free time, time at our own disposal to do what we like with. It involves choices. What we choose to do expresses something about what we enjoy and who we are. Leisure is for pleasure, not pain. Play, which is also crucial for children's learning and development as we see in Chapter 10, is defined as "moving about in a lively manner," "amusing yourself," "pretending for fun" and "being involved in a game." Pushing young children to attend after-school activities before they are ready or when they have had enough, and squeezing in time for quality play (not television), will do little to strengthen a child's confidence, self-knowledge or experience of self-direction. They do not have to discover every possible talent by the end of primary school. They have a lifetime ahead for this. A huge number of sporting, practical, craft and artistic opportunities is available to adults. Not every professional musician or sports person started young.

So how do we know when our children's leisure is giving them pleasure, when it might be in their long-term "best interest" even if they are complaining and whether they are doing too much? It is not easy; but we can start by asking them, or taking account of their pleas when they say they are doing too much or want to stop something. We can also inspect our motives, honestly.

7

Children Need to Be Noticed: Praise and Rewards

We all thrive on praise. It makes us feel good. I remember attending an aerobics class. There were at least twenty aging moms in the hall, huffing and puffing. I was trying to bend as best I could when I heard our teacher say, "Good! Well done!" She was speaking to the whole group, but I couldn't help feeling ridiculously pleased, taking her encouragement as personalized, positive feedback for my own efforts. Roy Hattersley, the author and former politician, has written something similar, recalling his best teacher and his awful first year at secondary school. It was a significant time in his life and he remembers it even now: "But I had one big moment in that first year. Standing on the hideous windswept football field where we played games, Derek Walker asked the class, 'What is the answer to quick passing?' and I said, 'Close marking.' And he said, 'Very good! That's right!' and even now as I tell the story and know I am boasting, I still feel the glow of pride that went through me."

WHY PRAISE AND ENCOURAGEMENT ARE IMPORTANT

Children love praise. It is one of the joys of living and working with children to see the pride and pleasure spread spontaneously and freely across their face, lighting it up, when they do something well and we show we have noticed. For almost every child, praise, incentives and encouragement are far more likely to produce the behavior adults want to see than punishment and criticism. There are various common phrases that express this: "The carrot works better than the stick" and "Bouquets, not brickbats," for example. Yet despite this, it seems much easier and more natural to find fault and to criticize.

Children need to be praised for more than just the pleasure it brings or its incentive effect. It is not simply a bit of frippery, an extra, the icing on the cake. It actually meets some fundamental needs. As well as being properly fed and clothed, children need:

- to feel important and significant to someone, to believe that someone is committed to them and cares enough about them to cherish them. They need to be noticed and to feel likeable.

- to receive clear, positive guidance about how they should lead their lives. They need to know what it is they should do, not what they shouldn't do.

- to be enjoyed and to give pleasure—particularly to their parents. They need to hear and be told that they have pleased them and that their efforts to try hard have been noticed.

Praise and encouragement, rewards, hugs, smiles and touches can fulfill these needs. Other responses from adults that achieve the same results are support, attention, appreciation and acknowledgment. We can show our appreciation and acknowledgment and reinforce the behavior we want to encourage, in more than one way. We can show it

- in words
- physically
- with our time and attention
- with presents

Children who are ignored and neglected are, by definition, not noticed. They cannot feel any sense of being liked or cherished. Children who are only noticed when they are criticized and reprimanded will not feel that they give anyone pleasure. They will hear only negative messages about their behavior. They will learn what they are not supposed to do, not what they should do, or the reasons why. Indeed, if they are regularly ignored, children will have little reason to be good because it will very likely go unnoticed.

Many people find it very hard to give praise. Some simply do not know what to praise. Some feel uncomfortable with the words and the general activity itself. Some are also reluctant to praise their child because they think:

- praise will make their child big-headed;
- praise should be given only for outstanding performance and effort beyond expectation;
- "normal" behavior and work does not deserve special comment;
- if something could be better, it should not be praised;
- a child should be doing well in every sphere before praise is given for any one task; otherwise a child may think that everything is satisfactory and fail to improve where "needed";
- they were largely responsible for the success by providing opportunity, enforcing a disciplined routine and so on;
- it has not worked; their child does not accept or respond to it, so they give up.

These reactions are very common. If we broaden our understanding of both what can or should be praised, and why praise benefits children, we shall find it easier to use it more often.

UNDERSTANDING PRAISE

Praise is about showing attention and appreciation, not judgment and conditional approval. Many people believe that praise is about telling children they are "good," which involves making a judgment. Work, or behavior, is judged to be either "good" and praiseworthy, or "bad" and open to criticism. But children don't want to be watched, judged and assessed all the time. They want more freedom than that allows. Children flourish with praise not because they are thought to be "good," but because it means their efforts have been noticed and someone has thought them important enough to pay attention. The words we use for praise and the times we give it should reflect our attention and appreciation, not judgment and occasional approval.

Praise is also about giving encouragement and accurate feedback. Many people think that praise is always good, or positive, while criticism is negative and unhelpful. Successes are celebrated, and often exaggerated, and mistakes ignored. This is not helpful. What children need is not phony feedback but accurate information about the strengths and weaknesses of their work that signals room for improvement, encourages them to be responsible for making their work better and helps them to assess themselves. Praise and criticism should not be seen as positive or negative but constructive or unconstructive. Criticism can be constructive—when it shows the way forward—and praise can be unconstructive, for example when it is too general, is false or hollow or when it sets standards of performance that are very hard to keep. We shall look at this in more detail in the chapters on managing success and failure.

What Can We Praise?

As well as academic skills, we can praise:

- the effort that goes into something (the process) rather than just the quality of the end product (the outcome);
- thinking skills, such as making choices, having ideas, using imagination, solving problems and thinking ahead;
- social skills, such as helpfulness, independence, understanding, kindness, sharing and resolving conflicts;
- physical skills, such as being good with scissors, having sporting skills and successfully building and making things.

The Language of Praise

Praise can mean both "approve" and "appreciate." The difference is important. "Approve" means to accept, confirm and commend. "Appreciate" means to estimate the worth, quality or amount of something, be sensitive to, esteem highly.

In other words, "approval" implies the wholehearted acceptance—of somebody, or something that person has done, without gauging or assessing why we find them acceptable. "Appreciation" follows an assessment, weighing something, attaching value to specific qualities, especially effort. Children need to feel approved of for who they are and appreciated for their skills, efforts and achievements.

We can show approval by saying such things as: "That's lovely!" "That's great!" "Magic!" "Brilliant!" "Well done!" and "You're a star!" These are most effective when spoken face to face, with smiling mouth and eyes and with an added gesture—a touch or a thumbs-up.

We can show appreciation for something a child has done by saying such things as: "Thanks for doing . . . ," "That was really helpful to me," and "You took a lot of time and care over that."

It helps a child if the praise is specific. Describing something in detail:

- proves you have noticed;
- gives relevant feedback;
- helps to avoid being unnecessarily and inappropriately judgmental.

The essence of constructive praise is information and encouragement. It is neither hollow nor false. It is filled with detail. It points the way ahead. And it should leave as much room as possible for the child to judge himself. This does not mean we should never judge. We can say, "I think that is good, because . . . What do you think?" which is very different from a blanket judgment, "That is good" or "You are clever." If children are to accept the idea of good enough success, they must hear it from someone else first.

Positive Comments That Avoid Judgment. "Practicing five nights a week showed real commitment."

"That's an interesting painting. I like the colors you chose."

"Thanks for tidying your room. It was a great help."

"Well done for being selected. You deserved it because you trained really hard."

"I am pleased for you that you got an award. I know that's what you hoped for."

"That model must have taken you a long time. Are you pleased with it?"

"That was a good idea of something to play. Thanks for letting Jo join in too."

Comments Avoiding False Praise. Here are some examples of things we can say that are encouraging but straightforward. They do not pretend that things are perfect, or even good enough, when they are not. They make the scope for improvement very clear and encourage the child to understand any errors.

"What a lovely story. I like your ideas, and the ending makes me laugh. I find that stories are always more interesting to read if they include how the characters are thinking and feeling as well as speaking, so next time, perhaps you can tell us something about your people's feelings and reactions. I know you can do that. Do you think you can? Good. I look forward to reading it."

"There's a lot in this report that you should be pleased with. For example, it's good that you're listening better during lessons and that your homework's not late any more. Well done. I'm very happy with it. I'm surprised, though, that you didn't do better in math and science. I thought you were more comfortable with them now. If you know what you find difficult, we can try to find a friend or neighbor who can explain it again before term starts. Do you think the report's fair? Are you pleased with it?"

"I don't call this a tidied room. You've done well to put all your clothes and toys away, but you're going to have to sort out that pile of paper and comics in the corner too before we invite a friend over. You can show it off to me when it's done, and I'll bring you a cold drink to celebrate."

"I am happy to take you shopping with me, but to be honest I wasn't happy with how you behaved this time. It's not okay for you to badger me constantly about having something to eat and then to nag about missing a television program. I usually enjoy your company, but I won't take you again if there's going to be a repeat performance."

"This is much better. Well done! You got twelve math problems right this time, which is much better than eight last time. Have a look at the four I've marked as wrong. See if you're making the same kind of mistake each time."

Self-Praise: Avoiding Conceit

Children are more likely to become independent learners when they feel comfortable with themselves and are able to assess their work honestly, praising themselves when it is due. Praising yourself is often considered arrogant, big-headed or conceited, so we are reluctant to do it. Many people think praising their child could make him cocky. However, children deserve to be praised if they do well or have tried hard, and they have to hear it from others if they are to be able to do it for themselves.

To avoid making our child conceited, we can separate clearly the person from what the person has done. His achievements may be impressive, but they should not make us value him as an individual any more or less. As soon as the two become confused we enter dangerous territory, especially if our own self-esteem comes to depend on his activities and achievements. If any child begins to brag unduly about his achievements, it may be because this is the only way he can value himself and feel accepted by others.

BRIBES, REWARDS AND INCENTIVES

Discussions between parents about the benefits of praise and its limitations usually come around to the subject of rewards, and the differences between incentives, rewards and bribes. It is helpful to look at the differences. We can then understand better how they can be misused and become a bone of contention, with children trying to negotiate bigger and better rewards before they agree to something.

Bribes

A bribe is an inducement offered to persuade someone to do something illegal or wrong. When parents use the word, they usually mean an inducement to get their child to do something legal and desirable that otherwise he would not do. "Bribe," in this context, is not really correct. The appropriate term is incentive, which is quite legitimate.

Rewards

A reward, according to the dictionary, is a "return or recompense for service or merit." When we offer someone a reward, we might say, "This will be hard for you. When you've tried it, I'll show you that I appreciate your effort."

Rewards come in three forms:

- social rewards, such as verbal praise and time and attention, which may involve a special outing
- material rewards, based on money and what it buys, such as presents and sweets, or even money itself
- nonmaterial treats, such as staying up later than usual, having a friend stay over to play, doing favored or responsible errands for the teacher, being relieved from a chore, going to the park or swimming pool or, if the child is older, having use of the family car

Praise, therefore, is the adult saying something. It shows we have given our child our attention. But we can also give something else of ourselves—our time, which is an increasingly precious commodity, to talk, play, generally be around or go out together.

A reward can be agreed upon in advance, or it can be a surprise, given afterward. A renowned "father" of parenting, the American Haim Ginott, wrote: "Rewards are most helpful and enjoyable when they are not announced in advance, when they come as a surprise, when they represent recognition and appreciation."

Incentives

Incentives can act as the motive, or reason, for striving to achieve something, and it may provoke us into doing it when we otherwise would not. In other words, an incentive is usually conditional on some agreed target(s) being met, and is designed to act as a spur to effort.

Incentives come in different forms too, including the following:

- "Sweeten the pill" incentive: "What you have to do is hard, and I can see you are running out of steam. When you have done it, I'll give you something to show I appreciate what you have done."
- "Kick up the backside" incentive: "If you get all A's, I'll buy you a new bike." What this parent is actually saying is, "I'm not sure you'll do it unless I tempt you with something."
- Negative incentive or threat: "If you don't pass all your exams, I won't pay for your driving lessons" or "If you don't run this lap in under two minutes, you won't be selected for the team."

The first two forms are positive incentives, because the child will get something if he succeeds, even though the "kick up the backside" will almost certainly have negative consequences because it implies lack of trust. The phrase "a bike or a bollocking" suggests a prize if a child succeeds and a punishment if he doesn't. In this case, failure would result in a double punishment.

Threats sometimes work, but only sometimes. It is important to understand when they have constructive force and when they are likely to cause resentment and backfire. They are more likely to work where:

- the target is achievable, and one the child would choose for himself and has not had foisted on him;

- the child has complete control over his performance and outcome;
- the threat, or consequence, is relevant to the task under discussion.

When Rewards and Incentives Backfire

Rewards and incentives can backfire, or distort motivation, for five reasons.

1. People can become controlled by rewards and incentives. Dr. Howard Hall, Principle Lecturer in Sports Psychology at De Montfort University, explained:

> You can get people to do things through public recognition and incentives—giving them certificates, writing their names up on public boards if they are slower than a certain speed, and so on. But their behavior will not reflect what is going on in their minds or their emotional responses. In one study, operating just such a technique, a group of swimmers increased their standards by 27 percent. Incentives and threats seemed to work. However, nobody asked them why they stayed in the studied group. The reality was that they didn't want to face public humiliation and public identification, not because they wanted to improve. People can become controlled by the rewards, and end up continuing their sport for the wrong reasons. Some footballers, now, won't get out of bed unless they get paid a certain amount. This is not what sport is about.

Children can become reward and praise hungry too. It can happen either if they receive too much of the wrong sort of praise or if they get none. If they develop an appetite for praise, they will not develop their own personal goals; they will lead their lives according to other people's values and not their own; they will always be looking over their shoulder at what others think, and try to please and appease; they will constantly think there is something wrong with their performance and feel inadequate if praise is not forthcoming; and they will become unable to motivate themselves when the attention or rewards are withdrawn.

Healthy praise and acknowledgment are therefore necessary for the full development of moral awareness. We are far more likely to become inappropriately dependent on praise and rewards if the approval of the key people in our lives is conditional, when we are accepted only for what we can do—when we succeed in some field or other—not for who we are.

2. When children are offered rewards and incentives, it prevents them from achieving something for themselves. In effect, the success is stolen from them because they are never able to prove they did it on their own, for their own benefit and for themselves only. Somebody I know expressed her fury at her father, who years earlier not only promised her $100 for every A grade achieved but also required her to pay him an amount for each grade she fell below an A. She got her three A's, but she has still not forgiven him for interfering and staining her success.

3. Incentives can reinforce bad or lazy behavior. Children have to continue to be bad to justify and ensure the continued supply of incentives. As Haim Ginott wrote, a child will be seduced into thinking, "I get what I want by keeping my mother thinking I'll be bad. Of course, I have to be bad often enough to convince her that she is not paying me for nothing."

4. Children can start to negotiate their reward and up the ante. This can easily happen with star charts or sticker-based incentives. We can begin the process as a helpful gesture, with a warm heart. We want to give them something, to make it easier and even fun. But then it turns nasty, for example, "That deserves two stars, not one" or "I'll do it for $20, not $10," and we end up feeling exploited. Why? Probably for three reasons. First, we can all get greedy. Second, where things become measured by money and expensive gifts, children will feel the bigger the present, the more they are loved. Third, it gives a child power. To argue and negotiate is an obvious way for a child to take control of a situation in which he feels manipulated by the parent's power to control him through money or other goodies.

5. When threats or incentives break basic rules of fairness, where the target is either unwanted or unreasonable, where the

threatened punishment is irrelevant to the task or overpunitive, or where a child does not see how he can be certain of reaching the target, regardless of his effort, he is quite likely to weigh these factors, feel insulted and resentful and decide not to cooperate. Children of parents who habitually issue threats will have their standard responses. Many will simply ignore the threat and their own potential in the process. Any additional stick waved over work and achievement will probably produce the same outcome, failing totally as a spur to effort.

KEEP PRAISE CONSTRUCTIVE

Praising children does not always have the desired effect. Most of us will have had, at some time or other, our kind words thrown back at us. "What do you mean? It's awful!" "No, I don't. I look terrible!" and "It's a horrid picture" are some familiar responses. The problem can lie:

- with the messenger: he is not trusted, not respected or he is feared;
- within the message: it is false, unqualified, given too readily, is manipulative or it is double-edged;
- within the child: he has low self-esteem, feels defensive or has clear views that differ.

When children have a very low opinion of themselves, they find it hard to accept anything positive said about them. They don't believe the compliments, and their defenses are so strong that they will not allow themselves to be "taken in" by what they see as undeserved flattery. Every comment will be inspected for the slightest sign of either insincerity or qualification to allow them to reject it. For further comments on this difficulty, see Chapter 19.

THE TEN PRINCIPLES OF CONSTRUCTIVE PRAISE

1. Praise the person rather than the deed.

Children need to be approved of for who they are, regardless of what they can do, and appreciated for their ability to manage any particular thing. If parents only accept and approve of their child when he shows talent and succeeds, they can create a treadmill of perfection for their child.

2. Praise the process rather than the product.

When children are young, the process of trying is crucial. They cannot write, draw or manage math perfectly. At the beginning, what they produce matters less than the learning process. Later, however, it does matter. If something is wrong or not good enough, it is just that. Constructive criticism signals the way forward and acknowledges and appreciates the efforts made by the child to that point.

3. Make it mean something—be specific.

Describe in some detail what it is a child has done that is pleasing, so the child knows exactly what it is he has done right and what he should do again.

4. Don't qualify it; say it straight—and with no sarcasm.

For best effect, praise should be given straight, with no if's or but's, no sarcasm, no reminders of past failures or other putdowns to dilute its effect. "You did well—surprising for an idiot!" or "This homework is good. Why haven't you done such good work before?" would negate any positive effect the praise might have.

5. Keep it honest and real.

False praise is as offensive to a child as it is to an adult. False praise blurs a child's self-awareness, undermines his trust in the adult and can increase fear of failure.

6. Keep it spontaneous; say it like you mean it.

Say it straight away and not as an afterthought. Say it to the child's face, not as you turn away or from another room, so he can see your expression.

7. Don't forget physical ways to praise.

Touch and facial expressions can speak too. Hugs, smiles and kisses are important. They communicate love, appreciation and wonder and can seem less judgmental and more spontaneous than words.

8. Don't constantly move the goal posts.

Let the child's achievement, at some point, be "good enough" to deserve praise and the parent's pleasure and appreciation. The child can then relax.

9. Let the child "own" the success.

Don't say "Great, you passed! I told you that if you revised using my method you'd do well," "If I hadn't pushed you to go to the swimming lessons, you wouldn't have got this badge" or "She's a great reader, but I've read to her every night for five years." Let the child take the credit for his achievement.

10. It takes four "praises" to undo the hurt of one destructive criticism.

Research has shown that it takes four "praises" to repair the damage of hurtful criticism and unjustified blame. This is true for all of us, regardless of our age. Heavy criticism makes children feel bad, stupid and unloved. To preserve their self-belief, we must preserve that important 4:1 praise to criticism ratio.

8

Make It Safe to Make Mistakes

Mistakes are an essential part of learning, for all of us, and at any time in our lives. They are inevitable and are even important. It is vital that we grow up being comfortable with mistakes, so we are able not only to take risks and be creative but also to face and process what it was we did wrong in order to work out what it is we need to do differently. This is particularly true for children, who have so much to learn about both their own capabilities and the social expectations of the world they live in. I asked a primary school teacher in London's most deprived borough how he motivated the children in his class. Without hesitation, he said he first makes sure they realize it is okay to make mistakes. But adults too benefit from losing their fear of getting things wrong. A manager in the training department of a well-known company, when told about a few of the things to be covered in this book, said, "It's our biggest problem." "What is?" I asked, as I'd covered quite a few points. "Making mistakes," she replied. "We find it really hard to get our managers to move things on, be creative and use their own initiative, because so many are too afraid of making mistakes and getting told off."

When a child makes a mistake it is proof that he is having a go and is at the frontier of his understanding and is extending himself. Mistakes provide useful feedback and can be used "to illuminate the task," in Gerda Hanko's phrase. They tell a child whether he has understood something, worked hard enough or is using sensible methods or techniques. They tell a teacher whether his or her chosen teaching method has got the point across to that child, or whether the child is in the right frame of mind for learning. They can tell a parent whether their child is fully committed to developing himself in any particular area of skill, whether homework is being done in the best place or manner to maximize concentration, or whether something more serious could be distracting him. In other words, mistakes are outcomes—neutral pieces of information—that tell a story about why something has gone wrong. It is the story we need to understand.

Once the reason for the mistake is understood, it provides information for action. Nothing can be put right without knowing what was wrong in the first place. Most people do not realize they are making a mistake when they make it; otherwise it would not happen. If the error is not eventually spotted by the person himself, then the error has to be pointed out, for learning to occur. However, a balance does have to be struck. Too much unconstructive feedback on mistakes will destroy children's hope and belief that they are capable—the belief that they can do things well and make a difference. The trick is to let children know, in an encouraging, supportive and nonjudgmental way, what they can do to prevent the mistake from happening again.

ZERO TOLERANCE OF ZERO TOLERANCE

"Zero tolerance" is an idea that has its origins in industry. It was developed to improve the quality of manufactured goods, which regularly left the factory gates full of faults. More recently, in both the United States and Britain, the term has been applied more widely, first to business, and now to crime and education. Of course, as many children as possible should be able to read and write, so they can carry on learning and fulfill their potential. But it is troubling that, even in places of learning, mistakes or misunderstandings are to be seen as shameful.

Childhood is a time of exploration, discovery and experiment. Children are bound to make mistakes in the general business of finding out about life, themselves and others. If failure is not only tolerated but also accepted, it will encourage growth. The experience of failure is very useful; it teaches us what works and what does not work. It helps us to build up a large dossier, or filing cabinet, of experiences that combine to develop our common sense—that essential resource that helps us to adapt, survive and be practical when confronted with the unknown or unexpected. Learning to accept failure as a constructive experience helps children to realize that they can survive setbacks, and that these need not be crushing.

Children's mistakes will involve their:

- behavior—when they do not realize something is not allowed;
- judgment—when they do not appreciate when to stop;
- physical competence—when they try to achieve too much and drop, spill and trip over things.

It is important for children's development that they keep experimenting, exploring and taking appropriate risks. Learning requires resilience. If a child is punished, ridiculed for mistakes and failure, and if an adult's expectations are too high—so that failure is a common feature of a child's life—that child will ultimately create for himself a zone of safety. If, on the other hand, he knows that mistakes are welcomed as part of the process of pushing back the frontiers, he will be released to be open, honest and happy to try out new skills and experiences.

We need to be tolerant of our own mistakes too. Parents make mistakes—through ignorance of children's needs, through overconcern, through stress or marital and relationship problems, through having to meet other family needs which often conflict. If we can accept that we can get things wrong, and show that life goes on when it happens, we can teach our children by example that it is safe for them to get things wrong too. The more demanding and perfectionist we are for ourselves, and the more we are crushed by a sense of failure for relatively trivial shortcomings, the more we send the message that mistakes are shameful—regardless of how positive we try to be in the face of our child's errors.

Of course it is right that children should work to achieve higher standards when they are underachieving. Naturally, it is appropriate for parents and teachers to say that certain behavior is unacceptable and will not be tolerated. But unplanned mistakes are different from conscious acts of misbehavior. What is important is not that mistakes of learning are never made, but that they are acknowledged and lessons are learned from them when they happen. Within schools and families, there should be zero tolerance of zero tolerance for genuine mistakes.

CLONES, CLOWNS AND CLAMS:
THE THREE ZONES OF SAFETY

Children who find mistakes uncomfortable, for whatever reason, create safe retreats, or zones of safety. They become clones, clowns or clams.

Clones become someone else. They model themselves on a key person in their life, someone who sets themselves up as right, good and successful. This person is often very critical, intolerant and judgmental, measuring everybody and everything against themselves—their likes, dislikes, talents and achievements. They find it hard to accept alternative approaches. Faced with criticism and uncertainty, a safe course of action for the child is to become that adult—or, eventually, any other adult who is currently in authority over them. This is the route not just to acceptance and a quiet life but also to becoming something defined as desirable. Unsure of themselves to start with, in the process they lose themselves completely.

Clowns become jokers. Some joke only through words; others use ridiculous and challenging behavior to get the laughs. Children who are clowns are sometimes described as attention seekers as they seem to crave the spotlight. However, they are far more likely to be avoiding situations in which they have to risk being wrong. Ask them a serious question to test their knowledge or understanding, and they will respond, often instantly, with a diversion. Any spoken answer will be silly. Instead of risking being wrong, they will cancel out the risk by creating a certainty—a ridiculous answer. Or to avoid saying anything, they may behave badly, drawing the questioner away from the question.

Clams close up. They decide not to risk themselves at all. Clams are very reluctant to get into conversations and discussions, and won't volunteer answers. If they begin to close off their ears as well as their minds so that they stop listening, they will then stop learning.

Clones, clowns and clams can also cultivate an attitude of helplessness. They avoid risking mistakes by claiming they need help and guidance at every possible moment. They seek constant confirmation of their efforts. They seek help with choices. They feel safe only when someone is physically or metaphorically holding their hand. This "learned helplessness," as it is generally called, is the opposite of the self-direction needed for self-motivation. If a child tends to behave in any of these ways, the best response is to build his self-belief and help him to realize that it is okay to take risks and to make mistakes.

LYING AND CHEATING

Anyone who is loath to make mistakes will also be reluctant to admit to having made any. He is far more inclined to lie and to cheat. Clones, clowns and clams are especially open to this temptation. Clones and clams will sit on their secret for some time, keeping things to themselves. Clowns may soon declare them, but in a flaunting manner as if to challenge, rather than as an act of contrition, because that is their style.

Lying, cheating, being secretive and stealing are related activities that often have complicated explanations. In simple terms, children lie:

- to get themselves out of trouble;
- to present a different image of themselves (pretending they are something they are not);

- to maintain a fantasy they have developed about themselves or their life;
- to avoid facing up to an unpleasant truth;
- to "play" with others: to manipulate and confuse—and thereby control—them.

Cheating is a form of lying. Children cheat because:

- their self-esteem depends on success—they cannot accept any failure;
- they cannot accept the consequences of their behavior (no revision or practice);
- they are only acceptable to others if they succeed in those people's terms;
- they want the promised reward very badly.

Cheating gives children no relevant feedback. Lying denies the mistake. They are both forms of pretence that prevent progress.

How Should Parents React?

When we discover that our child is cheating, lying or keeping important issues secret, it is, of course, distressing. We feel angry and ashamed. But it will not help to raise the roof. This will only make matters worse and prove to the child that he was right at least to try to keep things quiet. I heard the mother of a "problem" child say in a radio interview, "You can't get them to tell the truth by roaring at them or smacking them. They'll tell the truth if you sit down and talk to them. That's the only way." So we have to be calm, and we have to get to the root of the problem to keep it from happening again. In purely practical terms, lying and cheating prevent children from understanding and learning from their mistakes and from taking responsibility for them.

If we find our child is lying about grades or cheating, it is helpful to:

- let him know, clearly but calmly, that what he did was wrong;

- talk openly about why he was so afraid to let us know or to do less well than he wanted to, remembering to ask if it had anything to do with our expectations;

- encourage him to think about what it was he did that led to the errors (for example, not enough effort, lack of understanding), so it can be put right, making further pretence unnecessary;

- begin to rebuild our child's self-esteem and self-belief through the variety of measures discussed earlier;

- consider changes we can make to our expectations and reactions.

Make it safe for children to make mistakes and to take their time to master things. Enable them to tell the truth about their mistakes. Children need to be allowed to seek consolation for their mistakes, without the fear of being judged. Finally, always reward honesty about mistakes with understanding and practical suggestions.

9

Build Confidence
Through Competence

Competence means the ability to manage something. When we feel competent and capable, our confidence increases. Confidence means "firm trust, an assured expectation or boldness." It also means having faith. When we are confident, we trust ourselves and firmly expect that we can cope. Our faith is based largely on past experience. So the bottom line is: children have to be given the chance to manage things for themselves and try themselves out if they are to become competent and feel confident.

Children's self-belief is also rooted in our confidence that they are capable. The more we do for our children, the more they get the opposite message and the less chance they get to manage themselves, practice tasks and get better at them. Of course there is a balance to be struck. If we expect, for example, a seven-year-old to prepare his own lunch, he will probably think we do not care because we are asking too much of him. Children therefore need appropriate independence and responsibility to find out what they can do.

We have already looked at a wide variety of things children can try their hand at to develop new skills and competencies. Those who live in urban areas often have a vast array of after-school, weekend and holiday activities available locally, if they can be afforded. Schools are increasingly offering after-school clubs on-site, and find that these have a positive effect on their students' motivation. This is no doubt partly because students are feeling more positive toward school, and partly because the discovery of new talents is boosting their confidence. This chapter looks at how competence and self-direction can be encouraged day by day, from early childhood onward, in a range of ways. Not only do "self-help" skills increase autonomy and personal confidence; they also encourage a self-respect and independence that is vital for self-directed learning.

ENCOURAGING SELF-DIRECTION

Children can be helped to manage certain things for themselves from an early age. When they are very young, they have an unstoppable drive to become independent, to gain some control over their life. They can be ferocious when they reject adult help. If we stop them from trying, or show frustration or disapproval at their clumsy efforts, we may damage their growing sense of autonomy and undermine their belief in themselves.

In Charge of Themselves

Self-direction can be encouraged in stages. The process can be represented by five circles, each one inside the other. The smallest circle is the child himself. Gradually, his responsibility will extend outward to other spheres.

First, then, children can be given the chance to manage their bodies—feeding, toileting and washing themselves, brushing their teeth and hair and getting dressed.

Second, as they become more independent, their responsibilities can extend to directing their own thoughts and play.

Third, they can be expected to manage themselves more generally within the home, taking on some simple domestic responsibilities, organizing their leisure time with friends within guidelines, having their own spending money, managing their own homework, getting their school clothes and bags ready.

Fourth, they should direct and take responsibility for themselves outside the home—get themselves to school or friends' homes and begin to shape their social life.

Fifth, they should begin to take on some responsibility for other people, at home and outside, for example, baby-sitting, helping to run any clubs they are involved in, undertaking more important household chores such as cooking meals or mowing the lawn. This will develop important planning and time-management skills.

Some years ago, a friend was faced with a dilemma. Her daughter was six and asked to join her older brother at a week-long activity camp. When the mother telephoned to reserve, she found that his fishing-based camp had no remaining places for six-year-olds. If she was to have such a vacation, it was to be elsewhere. She found out that there were places available in an alternative camp two hours' drive from their home. When told about the new situation, her daughter still wanted to go, on her own, knowing no one. Should the mother use her "better judgment" and tell her six-year-old she would not be able to cope, or trust her and book it? She let her go. On the fifth evening of daily telephoning, the youngster was tearful and wanted to come home. When her mother picked her up the next day, she was busy with her activities, not morose. In no sense had she failed. She had had a good time but had had enough. She learned new things about her abilities—and her limits. She asked to return the following year.

A boy was obsessed with electrical knobs, wires and plugs from the time he could walk. He was always turning televisions, vacuum cleaners, music systems and video recorders on and off, breaking some along the way. Friends and family were sometimes exasperated, but he would not be stopped. Realizing that she had been defeated, his mother stopped telling him never to touch plugs and taught him how to handle them safely, and why and when electricity was dangerous. Before very long, he had graduated from plugs and knobs to extension cords, which even went on vacation with them, and not long after to building simple circuits, making light bulbs flash and so on. When he was seven, his family's house was stripped down and rewired, replumbed and replastered, and he followed the electrician everywhere, in seventh heaven. At

eleven, he was now immensely practical and competent, re-
pairing neighbors' equipment and building complicated anti-
burglar devices. His skill in electronics keeps him going when
he struggles elsewhere. It gives him status and earns him respect. If his natural curiosity had been thwarted, and his
yearning for competence ignored, he would have missed out
on an important part of himself that has certainly increased
his confidence.

In Charge of Their Learning

When children can manage themselves, they are much more
likely to become independent learners and workers in- and
outside school. They don't need to be told what to do all the
time, which helps them to think for themselves and progress
faster. They feel effective, responsible and in charge, which
also increases their motivation. We have already seen that
"mastery" and self-efficacy are crucial to helping a child to be
self-motivated, to be willing to learn.

COPING WITH RISK

The story above raises a stark and common problem for parents. How much danger, and at what age, do we let our children risk in the process of becoming more competent and independent? There are dangers inside the home as well as
outside, though it is the dangers of traffic and strangers outside that tend to grab our attention.

Managing Dangers

There are many dangerous threats to child safety in the home,
including not only electrical equipment but also knives, scissors, stairs, high cupboards, hot water, matches, stoves and
even garden ponds—to name just a few. Older children will
want to light candles, fires and barbecues. Should parents
never let children near danger or risk hurting themselves, or
is it better to teach children to handle potentially dangerous
objects and situations safely? Children who learn to manage

knives can help to cook. Children who help to cook learn to cook.

Keeping potentially dangerous experiences at bay may close down possibilities and limit the growth of competence. For example, many families with young children pave over the garden pond, if they have one, to avoid the danger of a child falling in and drowning. Yet monitoring the pond and its animal and insect life safely can start an interest in nature that can be lifelong. Someone I know who built her own wooden kitchen developed her interest in carpentry through collecting strange-shaped pieces of wood while walking in local woods in her teens. Perhaps times were different thirty-five years ago, but it is not unreasonable to suggest that the freedom to wander and explore helped to build the confidence necessary to undertake the project. If we obsess too much about the threat of danger, children may become overly fearful of new places and new situations and will not trust themselves to manage. They will be less able to take care of themselves and less willing to "go" even when parents are ready to "let go." This has an effect on motivation. How can children have the confidence to meet educational and personal challenges if they receive constant messages about their inability to cope—even to walk—alone in the street outside their home? It is better to empower our children and give them the skills to survive, rather than cocoon them in the security of our homes. Confronting dangers and fears helps to keep them in proportion; hiding from them makes them grow and does nothing to help us deal with them if we ever have to.

Of course, some places are much less child-friendly than others. Living in crime-torn areas will change anyone's assessment of risk. In these cases, perhaps there is more need to encourage independence and self-direction within the home to compensate for restrictions elsewhere.

Reducing Risks

There are a number of ways in which we can help our children to grow up safely, competently and confidently. We can encourage independence and responsibility from the start and allow our children to develop common sense through experience. Traveling in cars or staying indoors is no way to develop life skills. We should walk and use public transport more with our children so they can develop road sense and begin to detect the difference between normal and strange behavior.

We must teach children coping and survival skills, such as always staying in public view and in populated areas. They must be allowed to learn to avoid back stairways, underpasses or subways; go out in a group and stay with people they and we know; keep their risk-taking in line with their physical strength and coordination; carry money safely—a small amount in a purse and the rest elsewhere; and plan ahead and think through alternative strategies.

Children must have the confidence to say "No!" In potentially dangerous situations, children may need to question and challenge. Those who are always expected to be "good" and who always feel they need to please, will find it much harder to get themselves out of danger, either with friends or with other adults. They need to be able to size up situations and trust their judgment; have the confidence to be in a minority—sometimes of one; be prepared to be unpopular; and stand up to an adult whom they may have trusted previously.

10

Make It Fun, Relevant and Bite-Size

We all enjoy doing things far more if they are fun, if they mean something to us and if we can see ahead to the end of the task. Commitments that seem endless or pointless are much harder to stick to. This chapter looks at some tactics we can use, including the use of computers, to spice up our children's learning to make it more palatable when they are finding it hard work or, dare it be said, boring. It also looks at the need to balance work with play so children develop in a well-rounded way.

Some people say that, hard as adults try to make things interesting and relevant, it is inevitable that some children will find some tasks or subjects dull and boring. Children, therefore, just have to get used to it. Doing well often involves slog. Life is not a nonstop party, and children are let down if we lead them to think that it is. Especially as they get older, they should be able to apply themselves when they feel disenchanted and not wait for someone else to make it easier by jazzing up the process.

Task commitment is, indeed, a crucial element in successful motivation. We have seen that children are at an advantage if they are able to persevere. The trouble with this argument is that it is fine for children who have a clear goal or watchful and supportive parents to help them through the tough bits. Those who don't are, by contrast, dangerously vulnerable.

First, they switch off. As a result they then fall behind. Finally, faced with an apparently impossible challenge, they opt out. It is not just younger school-aged children who need tasks to be fun, relevant and bite-size. Adolescents need this too, to protect their futures. Learning, though, involves a clear contract. If work is made pleasurable and more accessible, children have to do their bit and deliver. Clear and consistent expectations about finishing school and homework and handing it in, and close monitoring and self-monitoring, are also important to ensure all children have the chance to make the most of themselves.

PLAY AS WORK AND WORK AS PLAY

Work can be fun, and for most young children, it is. This is not just because schools and sports teachers have taken on the message that children learn through play and so present tasks in a lively and relevant way. It is also because most young children want to learn. More than that, those who are ready are desperate to learn; they are like sponges. They soak up anything that is going on. They get such a thrill from finding out what they can do and mastering tasks and techniques that they ask for work, even if it is not sugar coated as play, because they enjoy it. For them, work is play just as much as play is work. It is adults who think there is a clear difference between the two activities and hold children back from too much "hard work." But if children's thirst for knowledge and self-knowledge is left unquenched at this critical stage, they will be left apparently directionless, which will undermine their motivation.

At the other end of the spectrum, there are some young children who are not so ready to develop. They need to be encouraged to concentrate and apply themselves. Making tasks enjoyable helps. People who think that play has less value than work deny some young children the chance to make progress in a way that suits them. In warm weather, children may like to read and work outside. Older children often prefer to work alongside a friend. Special cozy corners full of cushions can be created to entice children to read. Colored sweets can make multiplication problems much more real. Odd and even numbers can be studied out in the street, with a child having to say what the next house or shop number will be. If you are stuck for ideas, teachers will be able to help.

Many children like to work in front of the television, though schools do not recommend this. It is almost impossible to think and write well while following a story line on the other side of the room, looking up and down constantly. If there is no other suitable, quieter place in your home, you might ask if the school or the local library has a provision for after-hours homework. If you show that you value quality work, your child is more likely to see it as important too. Think about how you could make learning more fun for your child if he has lost heart.

MAKE IT RELEVANT

A few decades ago, rote learning was the norm. Children used to learn math, spelling, poetry, foreign languages, history and other subjects largely through drilled repetition. Modern educators have questioned the value of this style of learning because, although some things stuck for some people, so much else was either forgotten or too abstract to be understood, and therefore of little practical use. Information that has no personal or wider relevance is both harder to learn and easier to forget. Rote learning has its uses, but it is most valuable when it is used to reinforce teaching that seeks to explain things and make them relevant.

People who are born with a natural flair for a subject or skill are better able to cope with the subject matter "in the raw." Those without that natural talent need to make sense of the subject in their own and often very different way. It has to be made relevant to them.

Most educators, and probably most parents, know the importance of making things relevant, but it can still be intensely frustrating when something that is blindingly obvious to us is so difficult for our child to understand and pick up. And when we do realize this, how do we know what to make it relevant to? What will make sense? A good guide is to start with what interests the child. For example, most young children like to eat. Anything having to do with food, candy and cookies will whet their appetite for learning. To start an interest in words and reading, the names of the food a child is eating can be spelled out in magnetic letters stuck to a fridge or similar item where he eats. You can then play a game changing one of the letters to turn it into another word, thereby showing something about the sounds of letters and rhymes at the same time.

As children get older, they like to know why they are learning or doing something. They ask why something is going to be useful to them. Foreign languages are now taught not through grammar and recitation but through likely vacation experiences. History is often introduced to children through a short study of local or family history. Course work often gives young people the chance to follow an angle that interests them. For children who enjoy computers, "relevant" might mean finding some software on the subject, as discussed on page 104. At the very least, we should take the trouble to explain to our children why procedures or knowledge need to be mastered.

MAKING IT BITE-SIZE

Any task is more likely to be completed, and completed well, if it is planned in such a way as to appear manageable. Children are easily put off by tasks that seem easy to adults but daunting to them. Breaking projects down into bite-size chunks can remotivate them. And most children will find it even easier to apply themselves and show determination if the stages of the project are recorded on a wall chart and can actually be checked off as they are completed, so that progress is visual.

Remember, bite-size chunks:

• help with personal planning;
• help with time management;
• help with organization;
• are an important tool of motivation.

The idea of using lists, schedules and plans can be introduced to children when they are quite young. We can:

- show their usefulness by example—with holiday packing and shopping lists, and personal reminder notes;
- introduce them when they have to put toys away—inviting them to choose which ones they will do in which order and checking them off as they are done;
- encourage children, as soon as they are old enough, to write or compile their own lists.

However, there is a balance to be struck, as there is in so many things. People can become list-dependent. We need to be able to cope in emergencies when we don't have time to write lists, and to be most effective, plans need to be "owned" by the person carrying them out. Lists written by parents for children can undermine their sense of being competent and trusted. There is also a danger that parents will go too far in mapping out things for their children, at the expense of children learning through their own experience.

MAKING IT BYTE-SIZE: USING COMPUTERS

Computers can be great fun, and not just for the games that can be played on them. It is exciting simply exploring what they can do and feeling in charge. Children are naturals at computers. Once they get over the first hurdle of how to start, they are in tune with the technology, which can be part of the appeal. It's one of the few areas where they often know more than adults, and it makes them feel good. Computers may be fun, but what effect can they have on children's motivation?

The answer almost certainly is that it depends on how they are used. There are many good educational software packages that develop children's logical thought, decision-making and reasoning skills, as well as others that focus on reading, spelling and math. For children with learning problems, there are particular advantages. Computers give children the chance to: change, correct and develop work, so mistakes can be managed and don't require complete rewrites; experiment in freedom; be tutored by something nonjudgmental and with infinite patience; and present work in an exciting way, using sound and pictures as well as words. In other words, the combination of gaining knowledge, developing skills, seeing their work look "official" in print, receiving instant feedback on performance, overcoming obstacles and being in control can help children grow in confidence. Any child who is computer literate will certainly feel more competent and able to use a range of machines and accessories. Computer buffs have a status of their own when they know enough to help straighten out their friends', parents' and even teachers' computing problems.

There are two possible downsides to pushing computers. The first is that their use needs to be kept bite-size, because children can get hooked. A primary school teacher told me she was surprised at the number of eight-year-olds in her class who listed cutting back on their daily computer game playing to half an hour as their new year's resolution. I wonder if they saw the television as a similar "problem"?

Children who get caught up in computers and spend too long in front of screens of any description can fail to learn vital relationship and emotional skills, through friendships and time with parents, and fail to develop a healthy range of interests. As well as this, any dependence on the instant feedback and excitement of computer games can make the classroom and the teacher seem boring, and their work skills weak compared to their games skills, thereby lessening, not increasing, motivation to learn in school or elsewhere.

The second downside is that using computers for noneducational games, either excessively or moderately, will not teach children the technological skills the curriculum states they should acquire. Some games are very sophisticated, and are sometimes referred to as "edutainment," but others have little to do with presenting information, storing it, communicating, handling and searching for information, or measuring and controlling external events. Used well and wisely, however, computers at home can support learning, help iron out problems, encourage independent working and new ways of thinking, be the starting point for getting a demoralized child back on track and offer hours of family fun if they are kept where everyone has access.

WORK, REST AND PLAY

No one can work all the time without becoming slightly unstable and a huge bore. In our work-oriented culture, in which lunch hours and even evenings are disappearing, not to mention regular refreshment breaks, we are pushing ourselves to the point of collapse. Stress levels are reported to be higher than ever. At work, people are now monitored and measured; made responsible and accountable; evaluated and assessed. There is no letup and it cannot go on. We seem to be in danger of doing the same to our children. To guard against the suicide rates of the Far East taking hold here, we must ensure that quality work is balanced with quality rest and play.

The Importance of Play

Children with lots of experience of play have a head start in life. It certainly helps with learning, at many levels, and with motivation. Through play children try themselves out and find out who they are and what they can do, so it develops self-understanding. Physical play helps children to become fit and healthy and feel proud of their bodies, so it develops self-belief and competence. Having fun gives us energy for the more demanding parts of our lives; and how we choose to spend our leisure time is an expression of who we are.

Children of all ages need to play, including teenagers. It encourages a "can do" and "want to do" attitude toward life because it protects, cherishes and develops each individual's natural:

- curiosity, and the excitement and wonder of discovery;
- creativity and flexibility, through exploring fantasy and solving problems;
- confidence, through self-direction and initiative, and because trial and error is safe;

- concentration, through the tendency to become "lost" in play;
- cooperation, through playing with others, and learning to take turns and compromise.

Play also develops the skills children need to do well. Games and play encourage children to:

- talk, making it easier to express themselves in words and on paper;
- read, where the games involve shapes, sounds, matching and reading words;
- use numbers, where children count, use dice or keep scores;
- write, through scribbling, drawing, handling objects and gaining manual control;
- socialize and reflect, and understand the needs and feelings of others;
- apply themselves, where games encourage memory, listening and concentration;
- plan ahead and organize, as they decide what they need to do to make something happen;
- problem solve and compromise, as difficulties arise;
- accept consequences, through clearing up afterward.

Play and Children's Development

As children grow, their play develops and changes. They begin by playing alone. They then progress to playing independently but alongside one another, moving on from that stage to playing cooperatively in pairs or threes, at about the age of three. Cooperative play involves increasingly sophisticated social skills, which very young children do not have. Learning to wait, share and take turns, and coping with rules and winning and losing are also hard. Children start to do this from about the age of four, though it can take a few years for them to become completely comfortable with losing in competitive games of skill and to relish rule-governed challenge. Some people reach adulthood without getting this far.

Adolescence: Motivated to Party.   It is one of life's unfortunate mistimings that adolescence coincides with critical school examinations. Just when "the system" demands that young people get their heads down and prove their academic worth, they are wandering about, wondering whether they are worth anything—sometimes going to enormous lengths to try themselves out and piece together a notion of themselves. They do this through friends and through play. They also use play to experiment with risk and prepare for their future roles. They will often gather in large groups, which demands even more advanced planning and social skills such as negotiation, compromise and team work. Younger teenagers will often have an intense relationship with someone of the same sex before getting used to having the opposite sex as friends and finally moving on to the traditional couple relationship. Work and other hobbies may slip in their order of priority, and their only apparent motivation is to party, but at least they are developing some useful organization and relationship skills in the process. Provided they get enough sleep and do not appear to be losing their direction through irresponsible use of alcohol or drugs, it is important that they have a social life. They cannot be expected to work all the time, just because we are worried they might not make the grade.

The 80:20 Rule.   There is a familiar saying that if something is worth doing, it is worth doing well; but that depends. It depends on how long it is going to take and what else could be done with the time commitment involved. There is another saying, or rule, used in management called the 80:20 rule. I prefer it to the traditional saying. It comes from an understanding about trade-offs between the effort and the result—in management-speak, input and output. The first 20 percent of our effort in any project is usually the most effective and can get us 80 percent of the way there. The more effort we apply thereafter, the less effective that effort will be. If we arrive at a situation where we have to put in 80 percent more effort to improve it by 20 percent, the effort is not worthwhile, especially if it is at the expense of starting some other task or active leisure. Teachers sometimes express concern about the amount of time some students devote to their course assignments. Grades are allocated in such a way that the 80:20 rule often applies. They wish their students would let up and, instead, have some fun to help them through this testing time.

Regardless of age, "quality play" is any activity that:

- uncovers, or builds on, an individual's inner resources for coping;
- develops powers of understanding, and therefore intuition;
- deepens and enhances the sense of self;
- offers scope for experimentation and personal development;
- enriches imagination;
- develops social skills;
- explores and expresses feelings, thereby developing empathic skills.

The Importance of Rest and Relaxation

Children need rest time as much as adults do. Rest is not necessarily the same thing as sleep or leisure; it means stopping, having quiet time in which to think, reflect, relax and let go. Sleep is time when, by definition, we do not consciously reflect, though we almost certainly do in dreams. Relaxing through leisure is usually interpreted today as rushing about, blocking out thoughts of work with an alternative activity. There is merit in that, as it can refresh mind and body. But winding down normally means slowing down, mentally and physically, to a point from which we can explore our inner selves and learn to feel at ease with who we are. This gives us a second wind, partly because we use this time to sort out all manner of issues, whether we are aware of it or not. We all need, in the poet T. S. Eliot's words, "a still centre in a turning world."

I have seen children struggle with problems—in particular arithmetic problems and with playing a piece of music—and, without further practice in between, return after a day or two to perform each task perfectly. Rest made perfect, not practice. The difficulty must have been mulled over, consciously or unconsciously, while the mind was resting.

Children who are on the go all the time and who are not encouraged to take time out are likely to have a poorer sense of themselves and less opportunity to process problems subconsciously. Rest regenerates. Perhaps this is why all the major religions incorporate a weekly day of rest in their rituals.

Encouraging Rest. All children need times when they do absolutely nothing. They need to be allowed to rest, so try to:

- identify their preferred way of winding down, and give them some time on their own;
- encourage them to do this, especially after school or other times of demanding mental, emotional or physical activity;
- respect their need for their own quiet space, even if they choose somewhere other than the family home if this is too busy and bustling for them;
- encourage times of quiet togetherness, as a family or between you and each of them;
- help them to know how to relax themselves, and not simply rely on other vehicles such as sports or television.

11

The Motivating Power of Choice: Encouraging Responsibility

Choice is a significant feature of life today. Most of us have much more choice about how we lead our lives than our parents did; and the choices before us continue to grow. Provided we have the money to make them a reality, we have a vast array of clothes, food, shampoos, beer, colors to paint our homes, vacations and television channels to choose from, to mention just a few areas. Our sense of fairness tells us that if we enjoy variety and opportunity, children should have choices too. Most of us want it that way. We like to please our children, to give them what they want. Having choice is a symbol of freedom and personal expression, and allowing choice is a symbol of caring.

Choice, though, is about much more than freedom, self-expression and caring. The very act of choosing makes us feel more personally committed to whatever it is we have chosen. We feel more involved. Having made something happen, we also become responsible for the results of that choice. Most people find this feeling of involvement and control highly motivating. Any child is going to be more inclined to strive for a goal that he has chosen for himself than one given to him by someone else, and happier about getting there his way

111

rather than someone else's way. Choice is a powerful motivator, but it must be used wisely.

In this chapter, we shall look at ways to use choice to increase motivation; use choice to encourage children to behave more responsibly; manage choices, because too much choice can undermine its value; and balance personal freedom to choose with the advantages of providing structure, obligations and routines.

USING CHOICE TO INCREASE MOTIVATION

A friend of mine fell out with her father when she was a child over how to do a jigsaw puzzle. It would be a trivial story if this occasion were not the moment that she separated herself from him psychologically and emotionally. He insisted that she start the jigsaw by picking out the edge pieces and complete the outer frame first. She wanted to work on sections that took her fancy and join these blocks together as they were finished. He refused to let her do it her way, insisting that his way was best. It was an empty victory. Was the argument over the method really worth the outcome? It certainly dampened her enthusiasm for jigsaws.

Howard Hall, sports psychologist, considers it essential to put people in charge of their own improvement, and let them decide how to proceed. "Improving skills is the target," he explained. "There is more than one way to get there and it's up to each person how he does it. People then realize they can enhance their self-esteem through their own, controllable, efforts." The England cricketer Darren Gough has reinforced this point: "Professionalism is not about everyone following the same rigid routine. Individual players require individual training routines, to suit both their character and their role in the side."

Joan Freeman, an educational psychologist, makes a similar point in a book on gifted children, her specialty. "So much research has shown that motivation and achievement levels go up when children are encouraged to take more control over their classroom activities."

Provided the expected results are achieved, it does not matter which route is chosen. This proviso is important; it is where responsibility comes in. If the chosen method is not working well, it should be adapted or another method tried. What works for one person might not work for another, so it is not usually helpful to dictate any method as "the best." For example, is a one-handed or a two-handed backhand tennis stroke best? Different players think differently. However, a child should not be allowed to stay with his chosen method if it is clearly not working, just because it is his choice. He has to learn to assess his progress and consider whether his approach is effective. Learning to evaluate in this way is a more valuable lesson for the future than reaching a target in the fastest possible time, on a route set by someone else. In any case, in the long run, the fastest method will be one a child understands, feels in charge of and takes responsibility for.

Using Choices to Encourage Responsible Behavior

Choices can be given to children at home to increase their motivation to behave responsibly. "You can watch television for one hour tonight—you choose the programs" is far more likely to get cooperation than saying, after one hour's watching, "That's enough. Switch it off right now." The same tactic can be used with homework and other evening commitments. "Tonight's a piano practice night. You can do it before dinner or after. Which would you prefer?" Similarly, if television seems to expand to fill apparently infinite time available, a useful tactic is to suggest that your child write down a schedule for the evening, to include his favorite television programs and dinner. Deciding what he is going to do and when not only makes him feel in charge, less burdened by commitments and more responsible for delivering, it also teaches important time-management and planning skills.

Choices and Consequences

Behaving responsibly means more than being "good." It means thinking through the consequences of behavior—what happens if and when—and accepting that we have a choice, that we play a part in and contribute to what happens. This is something children develop over time. They cannot think ahead when they are young. Gradually they learn the difference between acceptable and unacceptable behavior, and after that they are able to think further ahead to long-term consequences.

We can encourage children to become aware of consequences through making it clear that they have a choice about how to behave and spelling out the implications. For example, "You have a choice. You can either do you homework now and be free to play with Darren after dinner, or you can watch television now, leaving your homework until later and skip playing with Darren. Which is it to be? I'll give you three minutes to think about it." Alternatively, we can say, "When you have done your homework, then you can play." This is matter of fact. Choices must not be presented as a threat. "If you don't do your homework, then you will have to stay in" may come across as a challenge and might be ignored. Staying in will be seen as a punishment rather than a consequence of a child's own choice for which he must take responsibility.

Learning to Wait

The suggestions so far have involved giving children a choice about how something is achieved—in other words, about the means. Children can also be involved in choosing what they want to have or achieve, which is about ends. Here we have to be a little more careful. It does not always benefit their motivation if they get things too easily.

If we choose something, it usually means we want it. The more we want it, the harder we are going to work to get it. Choice, then, is about wanting. But it is often hard to decide how badly children want something. Young children, especially, are renowned for wanting almost everything very, very badly, now. They have neither patience nor judgment. You buy them what it is they can't bear to be without, and then, after two days, they have forgotten they own it. When they get a bit older, there is nothing more frustrating than to respond to their pleadings, sign them up for this activity or that and buy the required outfit or equipment, to find that after one term they have lost interest. It is part of all children's development that they must learn first to wait, and then to judge—whether it is a wise purchase, good value for money, something that is worth doing, something that they will enjoy and so on. Learning to wait is important. Impulsive behavior often gets us into trouble even though, in moderation, it can be fun and exciting. For most of us, it is only after we have wanted something for a while that we realize how badly we want it.

As we saw in Chapters 3 and 5, self-motivation and achievement involve thinking ahead and being able to plan and wait for the prize of success: putting up with short-term pain for long-term gain. If we want something very badly, it does not necessarily mean we should get it quicker. It might mean we should be content to wait for it, and then we really know. In my childhood this was called "delayed gratification." It was thrown out in the 1960s by children who felt stifled by it, a rejection reinforced by a well-known credit card company whose slogan was "Take the waiting out of wanting." We may be helping children's self-motivation and self-discipline if we start to put the waiting back into wanting for choices about certain wants or goals.

KEEPING CHOICES MANAGEABLE

Children need choices to become responsible and to discover themselves, but they still need limits. The choices offered should be appropriate and managed, because too many choices can be worse than not enough.

The great thing about choice is that it helps children to:

- develop their self-image and identity, because choice clarifies what they do and do not like;
- accept restrictions elsewhere, because they do not feel put upon all the time;
- become responsible for their behavior, because if they choose to behave inappropriately, knowing it to be wrong, then they must accept the consequences of that decision.

Too much choice, though, can undermine each of these advantages. Too many choices can make children:

- feel insecure, through having too much control;
- develop little sense of personal priority or judgment, because they can have everything;
- become intolerant of any restrictions, anywhere;
- become insensitive to other people's needs, and unwilling ever to take a back seat;
- lose sight of the boundaries and limits to acceptable behavior, because the boundaries become fudged;
- take less responsibility for choices and actions, because unpleasant consequences can be sidestepped with another choice—"Whoops! Sorry, wrong choice; I meant this one."

Choices can be managed by offering a few, suitable ones. For example, "Would you like to come out with us or go to Jamie's?" is better than "What would you like to do about us going out?" because it closes the option of staying at home alone if that is not suitable. "Would you like me to read a story to you, do a jigsaw or play cards together now?" is safer than "What would you like to do now?"

Where choices cannot be closely managed, which happens particularly as children get older, children may choose friends, activities or buy things we would rather they had avoided. What can be done then? Much of the time we can and should do nothing, for this is part of letting go, especially if they have spent their own money. As long as they fulfill their responsibilities to the family and school, and accept the consequences of any decision, the choice is theirs.

THE FREEDOM TO BE CREATIVE VERSUS STRUCTURE AND ROUTINES

The more choice children have, the less room there is for regulated and ordered living, and vice versa. Self-motivation requires both, so a balance needs to be struck. Creativity and self-direction cannot thrive where routines rule, where everyone is expected to do something in exactly the same way at the same time. But too much freedom about how and when things are done can mean they never get done at all. Children can be given so much rope that they hang themselves, as the saying goes. There are no easy answers. However, managed choices, which achieve freedom within boundaries, achieve good balance. It is hard to get it right, and most of us are never sure that we do.

The Motivating Power of Necessity

Powerful though choice can be as a motivator, we should not forget that necessity has its virtues too. If we have to do something, we tend to get on with it. This is not quite the same thing as being told to do something, though even this can work in the short term. If we see for ourselves that something has to be done, we are likely to do it more willingly than if someone else directs us to act. For example, "You're off to camp first thing tomorrow and you haven't packed yet. You'll need an early night and time to do any washing. When do you think you'd better start?" is likely to be answered with "I'd better start now."

12

Keeping It Sweet:
Managing Success

Any discussion of challenge inevitably raises the specter of success and failure. On the face of it, these two terms seem straightforward and different. They are usually seen as opposites. Success is when we do something right and is always good, desirable and something to feel pleased about. Failure is when we don't come up to scratch and is always bad, undesirable and something to feel ashamed of. They are certainly loaded with moral significance. However, the truth is not that clear-cut. This chapter and the next one look at the positive and negative sides of both success and failure—at how each one contains within it the seeds of the other.

Earlier chapters have looked at how children thrive when they feel successful, at how we can adjust our thinking to ensure children have plenty of experience of success to build their confidence and at how to praise and encourage. This chapter unpeels a few more layers. It addresses:

- the need to see success in relative terms;
- the importance of getting children to judge their own efforts themselves;

- when success can lead to failure, through parents' thoughtless reactions;

- the idea of "good enough" success.

We know the phrase, "the sweet taste of success"; we need to make sure we keep it sweet, and avoid responding in ways that may cause our child to lose heart, opening up the route to future failure.

SUCCESS IS RELATIVE

It may sound obvious but it has to be said at the start that success is relative as well as absolute. A successful result for one child may be a disappointing one for another who is capable of better. When results are compared among children, there will always be losers. It can be very limiting and dispiriting. A child who does not come in first—in a race or in a test—or is not "best" at something, is always able to view himself as a failure if he is so inclined. However, if a child's performance is measured over time, and viewed in terms of personal progress and development, "success" and "failure" are self-referenced and become neutral. They provide feedback on whether teaching and learning has been effective. For example, a child who is a budding athlete who runs faster than he has before but does not win a particular race is not a failure. He has merely not run as well as the fastest, and he must look to his tactics, breathing or starting techniques to see where there is room for further improvement.

It is hard for children not to compare themselves with others, and all too easy for parents to join in this often destructive sport. However, in the long term, comparisons demotivate and undermine more than they encourage. There will always be someone who is better than them at something, so any personal success will be marred, and if we show our children that the only way to judge themselves is against other people, we are telling them their own judgment is not reliable.

Most important, this kind of comparison can be made irrespective of how hard a child tries. He will get no detailed or constructive feedback on his own performance, which even the "successful" high achiever needs if he wants to progress and grow.

Of course, seeing others doing better can be a spur to greater effort. The significant factor will be the size of the gap to be jumped. The larger the gap, the more it will tend to reduce the underachiever's motivation. So often, parents and teachers hold up the example of the best for other children to follow. It would be far more effective if the especially pleasing performance of an average child were noted, making such standards appear relevant and achievable to the majority. Do we, in any case, think it is good to make every child want to be "best"? There is far more to life than being the top. As Martina Navratilova, the tennis star, said, "The moment of victory is far too short to live for that alone."

ENCOURAGING SELF-APPRAISAL

Because success is relative as well as absolute, there are many situations in which success has to be judged. We have to ask, Was it a successful outcome for that person at this point in time? There are often factors to take into account. Has he taken up the activity only recently? Was he away or ill for a time? Did he have long to prepare for the event? How does it compare with his previous efforts? Did he manage it all on his own? However, instead of always doing the judging ourselves, we should encourage our child to have the confidence and self-knowledge to judge the quality of his performance himself. Ultimately, children have to do things for their own satisfaction and apply their own standards, not rely on the demands and views of others.

We can help them to make well-rounded judgments. We can suggest that they pay attention to factors such as those listed above, and offer alternative views if they judge themselves too harshly. Although it gives us enormous pleasure when our children do well, we should always be on the lookout for signs of undue perfectionism, which can be very un-healthy, as we shall see.

WHEN SUCCESS CAN LEAD TO FAILURE

Both success and failure contain a contradiction. Success can lead to failure and failure to success. It is easy to understand the latter. Failure shows us what we need to know and gives us the chance to get it right. What is less obvious is that suc-cess, managed badly, contains within it the seeds of future failure. What can sour success? We have all heard of the "busted flush" syndrome, or burn out: people who were des-tined for a golden future who fizzle, opt out or even commit suicide. What might have gone wrong, and how can we pre-vent our child from becoming disenchanted? Three useful guidelines are:

• don't make your approval conditional on the child's suc-cess—keep the achievement separate;
• make sure he does it for himself, not for you or for anyone else;
• let the child take, and keep, ownership of the success.

Keep Approval Unconditional

Being a clever and successful musician, athlete, mathemati-cian or budding actress does not turn any child into a better or more loveable person. Children can and should feel proud of their skills or talents, but their sense of self-worth should not rely exclusively or substantially on how good they are at these things. They need to be loved, unconditionally and at all times, for who they are, not only when they do well. We must separate the achievement from the person.

In Chapter 7, on praise, the approach recommended was to approve of our child for who he is and appreciate him for his talents and efforts. No child should suffer the burden of believing that his successes are the only way to maintain his parents' love and approval. Sometime when this child is angry, he might decide to punish his parents by hitting them where it hurts most and opting out.

Who Are They Doing It For?

There was a television program not very long ago about the Covent Garden Opera House in London. In one episode, young hopeful ballet dancers were being auditioned to join a performance of Tchaikovsky's "Nutcracker Suite" with the Royal Ballet. After the final decision, the successful ones were interviewed. One young lad of about ten years old was asked if he was pleased. He answered, "My mother will be thrilled."

This is not unusual among exceptional, or even merely talented, young performers. To reach that standard, the level of dedication is such that parents are inevitably closely involved, ensuring practice, driving them—psychologically as well as in cars—watching them and constantly encouraging them. Often a lot of money is invested, in equipment and instruments, in lessons and coaching, in travel and even in lost earnings. It is, perhaps, not surprising that children lose touch with their own motivation and see themselves as the vehicle for their parents' dreams. When the young champion golfer Tiger Woods first won the U.S. Open, his father is said to have shouted jubilantly, "We made it!" In a television program about musical prodigies, a child psychologist warned parents against getting too involved and taking over their child's soul. The child must be doing it for himself and not for us.

If a child gets a great deal of approval and personal satisfaction from success, it can be unhealthy and even dangerous. It can lead:

- to the treadmill of perfectionism, having to stay at the top through constant effort, living on the edge of disappointment when success is not maintained;

- to a reluctance to take risks and try new things in case he loses his position of supremacy or finds out there is something he is not so good at;

- to a tendency to look down on others who do not have the same desire for success;

- to a need to look to others for approval, confirmation and validation instead of deciding for himself what he wants to achieve and be.

Who Owns It?

Which of the following might you say? "I am really proud of you for doing that!" "I hope you feel proud of yourself for doing that. You deserved to do well" or "I feel proud to have you as my child."

Of course, our child owns his success, but it is very easy to take it over and away from him. It happens in two ways, usually without us realizing it. First, we "own" the success when we use it to make us feel successful—to feed our own sense of self-worth. We become so thrilled by the achievement that we cannot resist running off with it and telling everyone else. Instead of seeing the success as our child's private affair, something designed to let him know how he is doing, we use it for our own benefit.

The second way we take "ownership" of our child's success is when we invest so much of ourselves and our time in the hoped-for outcome that we believe it could not have been done without us. Earlier, we saw that rewards and incentives can have a similar effect.

Which of the following have you heard yourself or someone else say?

- "He's a great reader, but I think it's because I read to him all the time."

- "You would not have got that distinction if I hadn't made you practice so hard."

- "I told you that you were a natural sprinter. That's why I signed you up for the course."

- "He's a great artist. He gets his talent from me."

- "Congratulations on making the team. Aren't you pleased, now, that I dragged you to all those training sessions?"

- "I'm not sure you would have made it into Harvard University if I had not promised you $500 if you did."

These are just a few examples of typical responses from parents who take some of the responsibility for their child's achievements and who, in effect, therefore steal the credit. Here is another little test of your "ownership tendency." If your friend's child does something notable, for example, gets into a favored school, wins a prize, comes in on top in something or is selected for the team, do you congratulate your friend, or simply say, "I heard Sammy did very well. He must be delighted"?

What Happens Next?

How might a child feel if his success is taken by a parent? He will feel not "ful-filled" but "ful-empty," not to mention puzzled and resentful. His first reaction will be to fill up his emptiness with another success, and hope that he is allowed to keep this one. Later, though, if he is always left empty, he will direct his resentment against his tormentor and opt out of success as a way of punishing that person.

Personal success should be seen as a child's, not a parent's, property. Friends and neighbors should not be told about it without first checking with our child to see whether he wants others to know. We may discover, for example, that he wants to tell certain people, such as the other parent or grandparents, himself. Asking a child about this matter not only shows respect for him and his wishes, but also indicates clearly that the success is his to use as he pleases, not ours.

"GOOD ENOUGH" SUCCESS

A mother spoke to me with some shame about an incident with her son some ten years back. He had entered a regional debating competition and had made it to the finals. She had coached him for the last leg, played devil's advocate and covered all the possible challenges and angles. She then went to watch him perform. Sure enough, the predicted difficult challenges appeared, but in her view her son fluffed his replies. Nonetheless, he won. When she met him afterward, her first comment was to criticize him for his errors. He was incensed. He left the room, silently fuming, did not return home that night and has not forgiven her to this day. She wanted him to be perfect when his performance was good enough to win.

"Good enough" success is not a cop out. It does not mean being content with second best when there is room for further improvement or giving up before an examination or a moment of public accountability. It does not mean being lazy, using the excuse that other things have importance in a balanced life, true though that may be. Good enough success is, instead, the protection against external and internal pressure—against demanding parents and children's self-imposed perfectionism.

It allows a child unpressured time before moving to the next challenge. It gives time and space to breathe, relax, savor the achievement, strengthen self-belief and adjust self-image. Good enough success is an achievement that takes us to the target selected and no further, to the final stage of the motivation journey when we are allowed to kick off our shoes, rest a while and feel proud of the distance traveled, even if it took us one or two days longer than we planned.

ACTION POINTS FOR MANAGING SUCCESS

Is this something you could do for your child? Try to:

- accept and approve of him for who he is, not what he has done;
- have realistic and balanced expectations;
- make it safe to make mistakes;
- see success as feedback, part of the learning experience, and ask him what he has learned about what he is doing right;
- accept his judgment wherever possible; if he thinks he has achieved something to be proud of, that is enough;
- let him experience a range of genuine challenges so success feels real;

- value different skills, not just those commonly applauded;
- let him be proud; acknowledge and share in your child's successes;
- let him own the success;
- practice good enough success.

13

Silver Linings: Managing Failure

All children experience failure—lots of it. A child will almost certainly fail at his first attempts at standing or walking, and yet he tries again. He won't master buttons on his first fumble, tie shoelaces straight away or ride a two-wheeled bike immediately, and yet he is prepared to have another go to master the skill. Why do these early failures not make children give up, even though the frustration can be intense, while later ones in other spheres of learning can stop them in their tracks and throw them into the depths of misery? What is the important difference?

The uncomfortable truth is that adults are often responsible for the change. How parents see "failures" inevitably influences how children define and experience their own "failures." Later on, friends, teachers and other adults will also affect their attitude. Parents cannot protect their children from the harsh outside for very long, but how we start makes a difference. Part of the problem is the current emphasis on celebrating success. When we place such a high value on success, and make such a fuss of it, we automatically define failure as shameful by comparison. If we can promote a neutral and constructive attitude toward both success and failure, and nurture each child's self-esteem, we will increase resilience both to setbacks and to the wounds inflicted by others. The crucial objective is to keep alive a child's self-belief and knowledge that he can correct the problem and move forward.

Another part of the problem is that, too often, we confuse two things that should be kept separate. The first area of confusion is the parent and the child. Our child's failure is his, not ours. If we feel lessened by his shortcomings, we are more likely either to punish or to ignore them inappropriately. The second common confusion is our child and his failure. Just because he has failed to achieve something does not make him a failure as a person.

Another explanation for an increasing sensitivity to failure is the growing trend in measurement and comparison against others. If we allow and encourage this, we can end up with a child who, despite a string of small successes, still considers himself a failure.

This chapter sets out the silver linings approach to failure. It considers:

- failure as a neutral concept and an essential part of learning;
- the need to separate the failure from the person;
- effective responses to failure.

BE POSITIVE

Failure, like mistakes, tells us something. It provides useful feedback. But that information will only be useful if the failure is acknowledged, if it is inspected for the lessons to be learned and if those lessons are internalized and processed. Failure, therefore, can be the route to success.

What Failure Can Teach

Through particular failures, parents and children can learn a great deal. For example, if the mistakes leading to failure are of the "careless" type, in other words, arbitrary slips, the failure can show that the child understands the principle or process being applied but was not concentrating. We then have to ask,

What stopped the concentration? Was it the television being on? Was it boredom, because the task involved repetition of something already mastered, or was it because the child's mind was focused on something else—on a problem, an exciting idea or the next event of their day? If the mistakes followed a pattern, failure might show some more fundamental problems with understanding either expectations or procedures, such as how best to "carry" numbers in adding and subtracting, or difficulties with a particular tense of a verb in a foreign language. Failure might even show that a target was too ambitious for this point in time. A child can see from the feedback what he needs to concentrate on, what he needs to understand a little more fully.

Through the general experience of failure, children can learn:

- that they don't have to be good at everything to be liked, loved or accepted, so it can actually strengthen their sense of security if the reaction is right;
- that failure is not the end of the world, that it can be survived and therefore risked in the future;
- to sharpen determination to conquer a problem, so failure can increase motivation;
- new skills and develop existing ones, such as study and planning skills, problem-solving skills, reflection and increased self-awareness.

SEPARATING THE FAILURE FROM THE PERSON

No child, whatever his age, should be told he is "a failure," or on a certain road to an empty future. Words that send similar messages are "idiot," "thick" and "useless." These are all terms that convey a negative, no-hope self-image. Worse than that, they are fixed labels that appear to lock a child into that role. There can be nothing more demotivating than to be described as a no-hope idiot.

We can all be nasty. We have no problem finding the phrases used to put a child down. Perhaps they were said to us when we were young. Perhaps we heard our teachers say them to others in our class. Perhaps we have read them, or even used them ourselves. "Can't you think straight?" "You're as thick as a board" or "Don't be so dumb" are commonly heard. It was not so long ago that schoolchildren who made mistakes were given a dunce's hat and made to stand in the corner.

These words and actions are a form of punishment and induce shame and humiliation. Shame makes us cringe and feel like curling up inside our protective shell, like tucking away under the bedcovers or hiding in a closet. Contrary to some people's view, shame and humiliation are rarely spurs to renewed effort. Instead, they inflict emotional wounds that fester and leave scars in the form of anger and resentment. Yet learning requires confidence, flexibility, openness, trust, self-belief and the ability to let go of ourselves and relax. Shame results in the opposite; it makes us tense up, cut off and doubt ourselves. Shame and humiliation, threats and degradation, disempower children. They are the tactics of people who exploit and abuse the superior power they have.

Failure and Punishment

Parents who are inclined to punish failure, either physically, or emotionally through humiliation or rejection, should realize where this can lead. Their child might be tempted to:

- lie about the grades he is getting;
- cheat to get higher grades;
- continue to work at the level he feels he can manage easily and not risk extending himself for fear of failure and the disapproval that will follow;
- invest all of his time and effort seeking perfection in one sphere, at the expense of either a normal social life or extending himself and developing a healthier spread of interests and skills;
- boast about receiving good grades to receive the approval he craves but end up only annoying people, being disliked and thus needing to prove himself even more.

In the wise words of educational therapist Gerda Hanko, concealing failure adds "the strain of pretence to the strain of failure and further saps confidence." She continues, "Failure becomes something to hide when you can't accept the whole of yourself, or when you fear the judgment of others, or both."

Punishing a child simply because he has failed does not help. It:

- entangles the child with the failure, so that the child can believe he is being punished for who he is, not what he has done;
- amounts to double punishment, because the failure can, in itself, be seen as a punishment;
- causes guilt and distress for the parents' disappointment, which can set the stage for emotional blackmail;
- ignores how hard he might have tried; punishing him when he did his genuine best to succeed, and when his self-respect has already suffered a heavy blow as a result, is counterproductive;
- may not involve a relevant "consequence"; not being selected for the team because training sessions have been missed is a relevant punishment, but being physically assaulted or grounded will have no association with the failure and is likely to cause anger, resentment and a decision not to cooperate with parents again.

HOW EFFECTIVE MOTIVATORS RESPOND TO FAILURE

Punishment and humiliation may possibly work in the short term, but they will not be effective for long. They will certainly not encourage that all-important self-motivation. If we do see the need to intervene when our child fails, it is appropriate and effective only if it reinforces self-motivation and nurtures self-belief, self-efficacy and self-direction. We need to respond constructively, sensitively and genuinely.

Responding Constructively

Failure, as noted above, can be highly motivating. Handled appropriately, it can be seen as a problem to be solved—as a challenge to be met. In Dr. Howard Hall's experience, failure can make people "roll their sleeves up and apply more effort. They realize that the only way to overcome their difficulty is to take control. They realize that their self-esteem is inherently controllable through their own efforts. . . . It is self-evident that each individual outcome is not the be all and end all of life, but for some people at the time it seems so."

At these times, any reassurance of the "don't worry, you can try again" or "I think you did very well" variety will have no impact. The appropriate response to mistakes and failure that knock someone backward is to put him back in control. Encourage him to understand what went wrong, to identify what needs to be changed and to agree to an action plan, a detailed and staged program for improvement. Sports stars will often study video footage of their debacles to identify their errors.

Responding Sensitively

We shouldn't always believe the front our child presents to us. Failure can be upsetting, however much he may try to deny it, especially if he had really tried, very much wanted to succeed and was not expecting to fail. Failure can make all of us feel disappointed, frustrated, ashamed, anxious and sometimes sad. It can undermine our confidence. It can sap our courage, rock our self-belief, sometimes to such an extent that either we pretend it has had no impact, or we don't even try to do well so we can pretend that if we had tried, we could have succeeded.

Sometimes it won't be the failure itself causing the sadness but what flows from it. For example, a low grade, a poor placement, a bad audition may mean that our child lands in a different group from his friends. Or the root worry may be being teased. If we can get to the source of any distress, it will help our child feel understood and accepted despite the failure.

When children experience failure occasionally and constructively—in other words, the accompanying lessons and feelings are explored—it helps them to understand more about themselves. The better their self-knowledge, the more aware they can become of their strengths and limitations. It helps them to be well calibrated—to have good self-judgment and accurate self-awareness. On the other hand, running away from failure, or being punished for it, increases fear, distances children from reality and leads to distortion and pretence. Nothing is impossible for the person who does not have to face up to reality.

When a child has a significant disappointment, we can:

- accept and understand his feelings, and let him talk about them; we should not deny how he feels or declare the problem is not as bad as he thinks;

- try to reduce the amount of "failure" experienced elsewhere; for example, go easy on him at home for a while;

- help him to have some successes to balance it out; make him feel competent and useful to you in practical ways;

- explain that failure is a cloud that always has a silver lining; ask him what there might be to learn and if he can see any compensations;

- make it clear that you love him nonetheless and that you are there for him if he needs to talk more.

Responding Genuinely

It can be difficult enough to give praise and encouragement when it is clearly deserved, but it is even harder to be supportive and constructive in the face of poor effort or work. As a result, we—just like managers and teachers—can find ourselves in quite a muddle over what to say when our children do badly. We do not like to rub our children's noses in "failure"—at least, most people don't—but equally we feel like a fraud pretending that something is fine when, in our heart of hearts, we know it's not true. Identifying what children have done wrong without discouraging them is a skill. We know that praise and encouragement are important. How, then, can we comment on poor performance in a straightforward and helpful way?

Quite apart from this, we often go out of our way to avoid upsetting or inflating the egos of any other children in the family who might be within earshot. If we tell one child he has done really well, will another child think he is not favored if we have not similarly praised him? If we tell one that he really has not done himself justice and could have done better, will that cause a brother or sister to tease and gloat? We are therefore very tempted to send mixed, half or even counterproductive messages to children. We find it hard to mean what we say and say what we mean. However, receiving accurate, detailed and speedy feedback on performance so it can be regularly monitored is vital to helping anyone develop and improve, as we have already seen. Our weasel words, spoken for the best of intentions, in fact make it much harder for children to take proper charge of their learning and development.

REMEMBER

When faced with failure, effective motivators put the child back in charge, show the way forward and leave the child with enough self-respect and self-belief to renew his efforts. Effective motivators empower children by responding constructively to failure. We can:

- encourage our child to "own" and take responsibility for his failure;
- help our child to arrive at the answers through his own thinking process and show him a way ahead;
- put him in touch with his own power to monitor and evaluate himself;
- have realistic expectations;
- accept our child unconditionally, regardless of how successful he is at any task;
- help him to feel comfortable with his feelings of disappointment, frustration, sadness and loss of confidence so these are not buried and allowed to fester and undermine confidence.

In other words, failure should be tolerated and managed, not punished. Failure becomes debilitating to a child only when:

- it is linked to a judgment about him as a person;
- it reinforces deep negative "self" beliefs already held by the child;
- he feels irresponsible and impotent, and there seems to be no way forward, no way to change the situation or no need to improve;
- he is not encouraged to take responsibility for his errors or misunderstandings;
- we feel the need to hide it, for this sends the message that failure is shameful;
- our child is permitted to ignore it.

14

Curiosity Rules! Handling Questions

Human beings have a fundamental need to make sense of their world, and it starts from the beginning of life. Very young children want to learn. They need to learn. They start in their first days by copying and by being curious. Babies don't stay lying on their backs for very long. They are absolutely determined to taste, touch, sit up, crawl, explore, stand up and walk, feed and later dress themselves. It takes great confidence to explore the unknown. Curiosity, about both the world and what we ourselves are capable of, is the springboard for lifelong learning. How is it that the natural curiosity, confidence and determination of the infant so often becomes dented? This chapter suggests ways to keep curiosity alive through to adulthood.

Curiosity means a desire to know, an eagerness to learn, inquisitiveness. It might get us into scrapes, but it keeps us asking and keeps us open to new information. It is an energy that fuels and feeds a lively and growing mind. It is a formidable self-motivating force. A motive is a reason, and what better reason can there be for doing anything than because we want to know? It is a self-generated reason, which means we own it. And because it comes from within ourselves, it is more likely to be long lasting.

It is vital that we foster children's curiosity. However, as all parents know, this is sometimes easier said than done. The first thing that stalls an inquiring mind is the widely accepted notion of the "good child." We send clear messages that we approve of "good" children who do not challenge or make trouble. But many of us are intolerant of all types of questions, not just the challenging ones.

"GOOD" CHILDREN DON'T ROCK THE BOAT

All children need to be noticed in an approving way. In her two-year study in Oxfordshire closely observing children in their home, nursery and school environments, Rosemary Roberts found that "babies and young children urgently need approving attention; that they begin learning very early to behave in ways that will please their 'important' people. For a child, learning to be good means grown-ups will be pleased with you. But learning to be good also means you might not learn so much" (*Times Educational Supplement,* February 2, 1996).

Roberts asked parents when they felt most negative toward their child. Most of them said it was when their child protested verbally: contradicting, complaining, whining and crying. Having to argue with their child was not pleasant, but they felt more negative when their children fought with each other, and felt most rejected when their children protested outside the home and therefore showed them up in front of others. Children commonly whine and cry when they want to be noticed. The other verbal protests, such as contradictions and complaints, show that a child is thinking and questioning. Roberts pointed out that when we ask children to "be good," it usually means they should not ask questions or argue, should not risk failure and should not make their own plans or talk about their successes and mistakes.

Answering back is one of the hardest things to tolerate. But protest is an essential part of communication. It is the substance of debate and discussion, which is increasingly encouraged in education as children mature. Without protest, children cannot form their ideas or learn to resolve conflicts. Children who learn to say only what they think we want to hear become mere reflections of us and are certainly not exploring themselves. But, once again, there is a balance to be struck. They do need to be able, eventually, to defend their position in a polite, constructive and well-timed way. However they also need to realize that there are times when it is appropriate to retire gracefully. They need to accept different boundaries and be able to bite their tongues when required. And we need to learn not to view their protests as a personal attack and react defensively and provocatively.

WHY IS "WHY?" SO DIFFICULT?

There is a strange saying about curiosity: it killed the cat. Irritated parents have trotted it out happily for decades to stop their children from battering them with questions, wanting to be told secrets and generally "being a nuisance." Today, we are more likely to say, "Stop asking so many questions" or "Why do you want to know that?" or we might respond, "Just because." These answers are, incidentally, far more directly insulting to a child than the traditional response, and far more likely to kill curiosity than ever curiosity is to kill a cat.

Children's questions can be irritating, intrusive, threatening and certainly demanding and tiring. More than that, they sometimes reveal our own ignorance, which can be uncomfortable. It can be easier to say "Go away" than "I don't know." Questions do not always stem from genuine curiosity. They can be used to get attention, to control and to direct conversation, which adults have totally dominated until then, as well as a way to find out things that puzzle children. We should not ignore these why's, but it is useful to understand the reason they come so thick and fast at particular stages of development. At two-and-a-half, children ask "what" and "who" questions, such as "What is the doll's name?" At three, they ask "where" questions, and at four, they ask "why," "when," and "how"—prefacing more abstract queries.

Responding to Questions

Certain questions will, then, need different types of responses than others. If we understand the different types of questions children ask, we can be a little more selective and sensitive in our responses and preserve our sanity at the same time. For example, we are entitled not to be hounded by questions demanding something we have just refused if we have already explained our reasons and listened to their case. If questions seem to be thrown at us just to get us involved and talking, perhaps we should think about spending more time actively doing something with our child so they get the attention they seem to need. Once children are old enough, the most useful general rule when answering a question is to respond in a way that helps them to answer it for themselves. This hands the initiative back to them, and in the case of questions that challenge and demand, it also encourages children to think ahead and learn to read situations and people. What sort of questions does your child ask most, and how might you answer them differently? Here are some examples:

Probing and Searching Questions.   *Why were the Egyptian pyramids built in that shape?*
That's an interesting question. I don't know the answer. Have you got any ideas about where we might look it up or suggestions for answers? What made you think of that question?

Trivial or Attention-Seeking Questions.   *What are you doing now?*
I think you might know the answer to that already. What do you think I might be doing?

Personal Questions.   *How many boyfriends did you, you know, have before you met Dad?*
There are some things parents are entitled to keep private. I don't need to answer that question.

Embarrassing or Difficult Questions.   *What would you do if I got a girl pregnant?*
That deserves a thoughtful answer. I need a little time to think about it. Come back in five minutes and you can tell me what you thought I might say.

Demanding Questions.   *But why can't I go over to Mick's house?*

I have already given you three reasons why you can't do that now. Tell me what you have heard me say.

I think you can guess my reasons already. Can you tell me what you think I will say?

Dependent Questions.   *I can't do this. Would you come and help me?*

Got to a tough spot? Have another try and you'll probably surprise yourself. If not, I'll come and help you.

Assertive and Challenging Questions.   *What would you do if I refused to do it?*

You may want to do that, but I don't think you will. If you do, you can find out the hard way!

Encouraging Curiosity

When dealing with 0–3-year-olds:

- let them explore and play;
- answer their earliest questions;
- get them involved with a computer if you have one at home; special software exists to exploit children's willingness to experiment with its use in a very hands-on way, even with very young children.

When dealing with 3–8-year-olds:

- encourage experimentation ("What would happen if . . . ?"); simple science books for children suggest activities that can be tried at home;
- introduce them to nonfiction books that are designed to feed children's sense of wonder and curiosity; these are often popular with boys, who seem to drop fantasy play before girls;
- model curiosity; ask questions about things that puzzle you ("I wonder why . . . ?") and show that it is okay not to know things but to want to find out.

When dealing with 8–12-year-olds:

- encourage self-help through the use of reference books, the Internet and CD-ROM encyclopedias when they want to find things out; public libraries are excellent resources;
- develop their independence gradually and let them begin to explore their neighborhood with friends;
- ask if they have seen anything on television that has interested them and that they might want to further research.

When dealing with 12–17-year-olds:

- the challenge for us when our children become teenagers is likely to be curbing their curiosity rather than feeding it.

ADOLESCENT CURIOSITY: EXPLORATION AND EXASPERATION

Adolescence can be an exasperating time for parents. Even if we accept that it is normal and healthy for teenagers to confront, be curious and experiment, it can feel distinctly uncomfortable to have the certainties of our life challenged. But teenagers' curiosity must be understood and respected. Most people agree that, at whatever age, life is richest when curiosity is allowed to roam. It is the sign of an active and reflective mind, without which we stagnate.

Curiosity stays, or should stay, with us throughout our life. Teenagers, typically, are curious about such things as:

- rules and boundaries: How far can I go? What can I get away with?
- adult relationships: Can I make my parents disagree? Can I split them or manipulate them? If they argue over me, what will happen to them or to me?
- their future: What courses will I take? What job will I do and, more fundamentally, what sort of a person am I going to be?

- their security and safety: If I experiment and explore and challenge, will my parents still be there for me and stop me from going too far?

- the strength of their own ideas, values and powers of argument and how this changes their relationship with people such as parents and teachers: Why can't they see things my way? Why don't they do it this other, better, way?

- their growing independence concerning their body: How much can I drink before I get drunk? What does it feel like to kiss? What will I look like with a different hairstyle?

There is a great deal to be gained from a teenager's different approach to the world. It keeps parents up to date and it can be fun. The teenager's friends often add further perspectives. Provided you make sure they are well informed about the pitfalls and dangers of experimentation, you should see the benefits of their confidence to explore. It is part and parcel of an open-minded attitude to life, which will help them to go on discovering their potential throughout their adult years. They may make mistakes in the process; it is virtually inevitable that they will. With their greater freedom, the scope and scale of mistakes is greater than before, so the potential for feeling threatened and let down by the mistakes when they happen is greater. Nonetheless, the message within Chapter 8 remains valid: you should make it safe for them to make mistakes provided they are prepared to acknowledge and accept the personal lessons contained within them.

15

Golden Threads:
Making Connections

Self-motivation depends on being able to see and make connections in a range of different ways. We need to be able to see the connection between our effort and the result. We need to be able to think creatively, sometimes making unusual links to solve an unexpected problem. We need to feel secure in ourselves and about the future, through having a thread linking us to our past and a connection to someone who believes in us. This chapter looks at practical ways to give our children the valuable golden threads that help us to make the most of ourselves.

CREATING CONTINUITY BETWEEN PAST, PRESENT AND FUTURE

Younger children love nothing better than to hear us tell stories about "when they were little," especially if they make us laugh. They have an almost insatiable appetite for such stories, wanting to hear them over and over again. They love to see photographs too not just of themselves but also of us and others in the wider family when we were all children—until, of course, they reach the age when anything to do with families and their childhood becomes embarrassing.

This sharing of family stories has a very useful purpose, as well as being fun. It helps to deepen children's sense of where they have come from and where they belong.

Each of us has a past, a present and a future. As we have seen, past experiences have a strong influence on who we feel we are and on our attitude toward what lies ahead. Motivation requires us to face the future optimistically, believing that we will be safe there and that we will succeed. Children who cannot do that will live in and for the moment, which does not move them on. The future will be safe when past experiences have been broadly happy, or at least faced, thought about and understood. Being able to move backward and forward in their lives will help them to feel grounded and secure. If, however, there is a part of their life they would rather block out because it was difficult to understand or was painful, the block acts rather like a lost piece of a jigsaw puzzle. Without it, they are not quite complete. Each block is the result of fear and uncertainty during times when they were stranded emotionally. It breaks the thread. If there are several such incidents, the missing bits can jumble the whole picture so they won't recognize who they are. How can we help our children feel connected to a continuous thread so they can use it to find their way back or take them forward when they feel the need?

Approaches to Try

As well as telling childhood stories, we can keep some items from their past, such as a favorite blanket or toy, or a special school report. Soft toys are sometimes kept for years, especially if they represent a valued memory. Keep one or two drawings, pieces of schoolwork, certificates or other symbols of their creativity and success as well. If we do decide it is time to clear out bedroom or family closets, even teenagers can be told it is understandable if they are not yet ready to discard certain items.

"Growth charts" can mark each child's changing height, and a photograph pinned next to each mark is even better, though this takes planning and organization.

Finally, talk about possibly stressful events as openly and honestly as possible.

CONTINUITY THROUGH ADOLESCENCE

Adolescence is a time of great change. As teenagers change and mature, the challenge for parents is to help them feel connected, to the family as well as to their childhood. Tolerance and patience are important. At all times they need to feel loved and accepted, even if we cannot accept or understand some of their values and reasons for doing things.

The changes that take place are physical, social and emotional. They can generate anxiety and confusion. Although teenagers stay the same person, they can feel a need to reject the old before they build the new. Adolescence can, therefore, be a time of emptiness, when there is great scope for outside influence as they try themselves out and experiment with who they are going to be. Ellen Noonan, a counselor who works with adolescents, has written in *Counselling Young People*: "The task of adolescence is not to kill off the child in a self-mutilating manner. Rather, it is to leave the child in the past as a memory, and at the same time to retain modified capabilities and qualities which were originally developed in childhood. Those qualities—imagination, curiosity and the capacity to lose oneself in play—are essential to learning, sexuality and achievement as an adult."

Leisure Interests and Past Times

In adolescence, interests often change and multiply. Previous interests may be given up, but new ones usually take their place as new possibilities are explored. Teenagers can be very creative and adventurous. Schoolwork often takes up more time, but this frequently offers students an opportunity to explore a personal slant. Teenagers may want to take a part-time job or have more time to themselves and with friends, so are tempted to drop previous activities.

Research shows that people feel more fulfilled and are better balanced as adults if they have a variety of interests outside work and the family, so it might not be good for your teenager to drop everything at once if he has no plans for new activities. Although adolescence is a quest for a new self, try to negotiate an acceptable commitment, or dropping the previous activities in stages, not all at once.

We can help our teenagers to feel connected if we:

- stay strong enough to acknowledge their different outlook and ways, and continue to accept them and be there for them;
- keep to the same house rules and boundaries, adjusted for their age;
- show that, within your boundaries, you trust them with what they want to do;
- try to accept some of their plans: "I'll support you in that but not in this";
- maintain a united front with the other parent if there are any arguments;
- keep the lines of communication open.

MAKING MENTAL CONNECTIONS: CREATIVE THINKING

Creative thinking is important. It expands our horizons and opens our eyes to new ways of doing things. It helps us to feel capable and confident because, if we are creative, we know we will find a workable solution to a problem even if we are not sure what is expected. It is fun, because it uncovers surprises. It is the thinking that generates jokes and cartoons and is the launchpad for innovation. Creative thinkers are original and flexible thinkers. They have to have the confidence to think the unthinkable and the flexibility to see unusual connections between events, theories or products, between one field and another. For example, the stethoscope was created when its inventor remembered tapping out messages to his childhood friends on a hollow log.

Children are born creative and resourceful. Many people believe they are more creative than adults because they have not gotten locked into set ways of seeing things, the pressure to conform or the constraints of logic. I recall asking, on different occasions, each of my children when they were still quite young to eat some item of food more "normally." One was eating a biscuit, the other a piece of toast. They both explained that their bites changed the shape each time and they were holding it up to decide what to turn the food into next. Edward de Bono, the writer famous for his work on creative thinking, produced a book called *Children Solve Problems,* which shows clearly how creative children can be. He presented children with a number of practical problems and invited them to draw pictures and plans of their solutions to avoid being limited by language. Some examples of the creative challenges he set are "improve the human body," "invent a sleep machine," "design a fun machine" and "create a bicycle for postmen." Any child can be invited to do the same, and the results will be as delightful and funny as those in the book.

Brainstorming

Brainstorming is a successful technique for generating plenty of creative ideas and solutions. In a brainstorm, four rules operate. These are:

1. Suspend judgment: every idea is accepted without criticism.
2. Freewheel: "normal" assumptions should be ignored.
3. Work on quantity: develop as many ideas as possible.
4. Cross-fertilize: build on other people's ideas.

Helping Children to Be Creative

Encourage games and activities that develop creativity and flexible thinking: imaginative play, painting and drawing, word association or word choice games such as I Spy and alphabet games and crosswords. For older children, computer graphics programs, role-playing and fantasy games, dressmaking, cooking, carpentry, textile or CD cover design and technology projects will all support creativity.

Model flexible thinking so they will follow your example. Talk to them about any connections you see between objects and events: "That reminds me of . . . " "That makes me think about . . ." or "Does that make you think of anything?" For example, it is quite easy to make connections between children's stories or songs and their everyday experiences.

Young children can get frustrated by the constraints of handwriting and cannot always write down the complex stories that are in their heads. You could either let them dictate their story to you or suggest that they speak it into a tape recorder. This is a good idea for long car trips.

Tolerate some messiness while the thoughts are flowing. Free thinking cannot occur when we are worried about being scolded for chaos or mess. I prefer to use the word "busy" instead of mess when children have been productive and well occupied. The aftermath must be cleaned up, but it will not help to fret about it before they have finished exploring and experimenting. Even better, think ahead and lay down protective paper or put a waste bin close by to calm your anxious worry.

Encourage younger children, or older ones who are strongly visual, to problem-solve on paper, using pictures instead of words. Give them the chance to use their ingenuity. Tell them what the goal is, and how long they have got to reach it, but not precisely how to get there.

Always value creativity. Kitty, the girl in Bel Mooney's books of the same name, failed in her attempt to build a plastic model ship because she was too eager to start and would not read the instructions. Undaunted, she added shells and an anchor to the collapsed version that she produced and instead created a shipwreck.

Help your children to become aware of the time and place that they think most creatively. Then they'll learn when and where to get the best out of themselves.

Don't expect them always to conform. If they are happy to be the odd one out, that should be okay. Don't dismiss or criticize an idea as silly. This may discourage their creative efforts. Instead, either ask how they expect this idea to work or ask them for three more ideas, inviting them to select the most practical one from all those suggested.

16

Cooperate to Motivate

Motivation is frequently marred by conflict. Of course, arguments are part and parcel of family life. It is not easy to live closely with other people in perfect and constant harmony. Children inevitably assert their independence and compete against each other. There are different interests to satisfy. Children want things there isn't the money to buy. Parents often have different approaches, which can add to the tension. We can all say things clumsily and provoke defensive replies. While it is normal and healthy for people to express different views, even to tease and banter, families that are in constant conflict hold children back. The challenge is not to wipe out conflict, but to avoid unnecessary battles and manage the rest without leaving a trail of simmering resentment. It is interesting to note that "grievance" is linked to the word "grief," which comes from the Latin *gravis,* meaning heavy. When we feel resentful, or "aggrieved," we bear a heavy sadness about losing something—usually an important person's support and understanding.

WHO DOES WHAT?

Take a moment to write down the things that cause the most friction in your home. It might be clothes, bedtimes, staying out late, spending too much time in front of the computer or television, what your children eat, messy bedrooms, inappropriate table manners, poor school results, not telling you about comings and goings or generally getting into trouble. If you have several children and a partner, write a separate list for each one. When compiling your lists, think about the following points:

- Try to prioritize. Which is your biggest gripe, then next biggest? The less you argue, the more cooperative everyone will feel. Rather than argue about everything and get nowhere, choose the two or three things that irritate you most, and focus on those areas.

- Be specific and positive about the changes you want. Looking at your priority areas, write down what, precisely, you expect, or would like, to happen.

- Be reasonable. Write down two good reasons why you want it that way—to check that you have a good case and to justify your request if challenged.

- Make it practical. Is your child capable of reaching your target (for example, putting dirty clothes in the wash basket)? What might he or you need to do to manage it better (for example, put a special bag outside his room)? How might he do it (for example, develop a nightly routine)? If your child is not old enough to think up a strategy for himself, you will need to suggest one and get him to agree to it. Would a simple reward scheme help to get the habit established?

- Identify room for compromise. It might be a good tactic to show flexibility, so think about this before you start talking (for example, having his own laundry bag in his bedroom instead of using the main one in another room).

Now present your plan for a more peaceful life. State your aim positively. You are trying to create a more pleasant life for everyone. Don't just tell them they are driving you mad.

If your children are old enough, and you feel brave enough, you could invite them to do the same. When you are all calm, everyone's lists and priorities can be discussed, and joint targets and compromises, with tolerance and patience, agreed upon.

CONFLICT OVER HOMEWORK, TELEVISION AND LEISURE

All arguments at home disturb children, especially those between parents or between a parent and a partner. What affects motivation more obviously and directly is conflict over homework, television and commitment to activities such as sports and music practice. Here are some guidelines and tips.

Homework

Children are more likely to do the work required by school if it is treated seriously at home. The need for time and space should be respected, with homework fitted into the family routine. If there is too much opportunity to avoid it, or not finish it, children may not learn the lessons of commitment, application and perspiration. Though homework is important, it does not help to argue about it. Arguments about homework are usually about four things: where it is done, how it is done, when it is done (and if it is done) and who should do it.

Where It Is Done. Homework can be done anywhere your child feels comfortable if the work is of an acceptable quality. Some children like to work on the floor, others at a table. A regular place helps to set up a routine. A flat surface is usually necessary for legible handwriting, using rulers and so on. Apparently, the British prime minister, Tony Blair, always works on a soft sofa, never at a table.

How It Is Done. Within reason, how it is done is up to them. Some like total quiet; others like company or some background noise. Short breaks may help to keep up concentration, but others may lose the thread if they stop too often. It's your child's work, and your child's teacher needs to know what your child does not know. Keep criticisms to a minimum. Don't look at it and think how you would have done it. If you see any mistakes, suggest that they check it again; or let the teacher do the teaching.

When It Is Done. Although some people work better under pressure, leaving everything until the last minute is not a good habit to get into. Rushed work can be careless work. Routines can help to take the tension out of wondering when they will get around to doing it. As children get older, they have to do it their way. Check with your child to see whether there is work due, whether it has been done and, sometimes, whether it was done satisfactorily. Ask to see it.

By Whom It Is Done. Homework should be done by the child. Homework helps children to learn to work on their own. The more you interfere, the less they learn self-management. Children need to be able to rely on themselves. If you take it over, you imply that they can't do it properly, and arguments are more likely. Research has shown that children can stop seeing work as their own if someone else does even a small part of it, especially if that involves writing on their work. If children are unclear about how to do something, try to lead them to the right answer through asking them questions rather than simply telling them the answer, so they learn enough to do it for themselves next time.

To sum up, we should:

- treat homework as important, and make it a high priority;
- try to establish good homework routines;
- offer some choice about how, where, when, so they feel in charge of it—provided it gets done, of course;
- agree on a suitable place—where possible, quiet and somewhere with a flat surface;
- show confidence that they will manage it well;
- be there to talk about it or look at it if they want you to;
- let the teacher do the teaching if, when you try to help, it leads to arguments;
- cooperate to motivate.

Television

Television and computer games are great for filling empty time and for keeping children out of harm's, and parents', way; but clear rules are needed about the time spent if children are not to get "glued" to the screen, ignore their work and, more important, miss out on chances to do other things and find out more about themselves. Worries about children's viewing and playing habits usually concern how much time they spend in front of the screen, and the content of what they see and do.

Issues of Time. Children need our time and attention. Time spent in front of television or computer is time not spent talking to us (if we are around), getting evidence that we enjoy their company and are interested in what they think and feel. Many children like to wind down after school in front of the television, but they can get stuck there. Research has shown that children's arousal levels can get so low after half an hour of television watching that they become overrelaxed—not a good mental state for homework. A television guide will help them to select programs and limit their viewing themselves. Invite them to write down their choices and their plan for the afternoon or evening's viewing. Research has also shown that children who watch a lot of television tend to have low self-esteem, be more antisocial and have poorer language development, so we do need to be careful about how much they watch. The more we talk to children, the better their language and learning skills become.

Issues of Content. Many parents worry about the suitability of certain programs for children. They fear that unpleasant news items will make younger children fearful or anxious and lose their innocence or trust in adults. They fear that violent and sexually explicit drama may lead to copycat behavior, desensitize children and reinforce a macho-style, antieducation culture, which boys, in particular, seem to pick up. Research that has tried to identify a clear link between watching violence and violent behavior is considered inconclusive; nevertheless, many people remain convinced there is a link. Most television networks have agreed to schedule material that is not suitable for family viewing after 9P.M. Preventing young children from watching after this time will be the best way to safeguard their development. Always remember that your own attitudes and values will have the greatest long-term impact.

To sum up, we should:

- try to agree on rules about when and for how long to watch television, and bring the total number of hours down bit by bit;
- help them to think of other things they might do, as nagging is not usually effective;
- sometimes watch television with them or, even better, do something else together;
- make sure they get plenty of physical exercise too, as this sharpens the mind;
- use television to develop imagination, judgment and other learning skills: discuss the programs, follow up on activities shown on-screen, invite them to think up an alternative ending to a drama and encourage other computer-based skills if game-playing seems to dominate;
- offer a balance of activities, as children develop best when they do a number of different things.

Extracurricular "Homework"

Children learn many different things outside the classroom that require extra commitments beyond the actual lesson time, such as sports training and music practice. Children often see these as boring and wish they were not necessary. The more arguments there are, the less a child will enjoy the activity and may ask to give it up. How can these commitments be managed so they stop being such a bone of contention, yet get done?

A child's age, personality, interest and natural talent will affect the rules and expectations. Some children willingly do what they are asked, while others fight every inch of the way, especially if pushed. Teachers and coaches usually make clear the tasks for the week and how much time they expect a child to spend on them. If the week's work is not expressed in terms of targets for improvement, there is a tendency to ask for a time commitment that will ensure a measure of progress—probably more than a child feels is necessary. Rather than push to the point of breakdown, it is far better, first, to try using some incentives and then renegotiate the child's commitment in discussion with the teacher if the incentives fail. Arguments over these extra commitments usually cover how often and how the practice gets done. The last resort before considering that a child stop the activity altogether is to change the teacher.

How Often. Be guided by the teacher. Short, frequent sessions work better than one or two longer sessions. With musical instruments, three times a week is usually the minimum to ensure progress. Younger children can be given incentives, such as pennies or sweets put in a "practice jar," emptied every two or four weeks. This can be enough to get children over a difficult period. Record sheets can work well, and help everyone to agree on what was done when. Regular practice is certainly valuable. It encourages stickability, demonstrates a useful lesson that effort produces results, makes the lessons more enjoyable and productive, and if it takes place at a set time, it reduces the scope for conflict. However, some children will apply themselves better if they feel in the mood. If they have enough self-motivation to be trusted with the flexibility, this is fine.

Practice Quality. This is the teacher's responsibility. Ask your child whether he wants your help. Sometimes he may, sometimes not. If he invites you to listen or watch—do just that; resist the temptation to comment or criticize.

Giving Up. Consider whether your child has given it his best shot. Whose idea was it to start the activity, yours or his? Would the money be useful if he stopped? Is there something else he wants to do instead? Might you try a different teacher first? Might he like a break and then go back later?

To sum up, we should:

- let the teacher do the teaching and don't expect too much; practice may make perfect in the end, but not every time our child plays;
- remember that praise and encouragement go a long way, so notice his efforts;
- agree on a commitment about how many times a week and for how long, and try to keep to it;
- let him say what is manageable for him, if there's a dispute, and keep him to it.

Lazy Listening and Careless Talk

An American researcher, Stanley Coopersmith, monitored the development of 1,760 children for seven years and identified three aspects of their lives that seemed to make a difference to their self-esteem. These were:

1. A caring, positive and supportive environment
2. Structure, consistency and predictability
3. Someone there who listens

Lazy listening not only harms self-esteem but also fuels conflict. How can we avoid lazy listening and careless talk, and instead foster cooperation and understanding, not confrontation?

Lazy listening:

- misses the message;
- forgets the feeling;
- closes the communication;
- starts and ends with the listener, not the child.

Careless talk:

- is directive;
- is deflective;

- is destructive;
- is dismissive;
- disempowers the child.

Listening That "Hears." Various terms have been used to define listening that "hears" and registers what is being said. These include effective listening, reflective listening, sensitive listening, active listening and attentive listening. Paul Greenhalgh, in his book *Emotional Growth and Learning,* defines real listening as when the person speaking is "being heard from the point of view of [his] own experience." In other words, real listening respects and accepts the world of the person speaking. Greenhalgh concludes that "effective dialogue is aided when the adult communicates that she has accurately understood the young person's frame of reference, which requires responding with empathy."

Communication works when an adult:

- wants to understand;
- mostly knows what the child means;
- usually senses feelings;
- appreciates how the experience feels to the child.

Listening involves paying, or giving, attention. We have to give something of ourselves. "Attention" means consideration and care. "Attentive" means observant. Attentive listening could therefore be defined as listening in which the listener is careful to pay attention: the listener is observant, shows consideration and seems to care.

All the different terms used to define productive listening entail important aspects of the whole listening process. So, for example:

- attentive listening refers to attitude, being observant and considerate;
- effective listening refers to results, whether the outcome addresses the problem expressed;

- reflective listening refers to the process of reflecting to confirm that we have understood;
- active listening emphasizes that the activity entails effort and is not passive;
- sensitive listening refers to the need, sometimes, to look beyond the words to identify the feelings and intended meaning behind them.

Listening, we can now see, is therefore a multistaged process:

1. Stop what you are doing. Mentally prepare; let go of yourself, empty your mind of your thoughts and imagine you are standing in the space between you and your child.
2. Apply yourself to listening and concentrate. Turn to face your child, look at him and continue looking at him even if he turns away.
3. Receive the message; hold on to the words, hear them repeated in your mind and mentally file them somewhere.
4. Think about what has been said and reflect it back, saying, for example, "So you didn't like what he said to you . . ." to confirm you have heard.
5. Check through your child's response that your understanding is accurate.
6. Absorb the implications, for you and others, of what you have heard.
7. Act accordingly, incorporating what has been said.

This staged process can be summarized in the six-letter word LISTEN.

L stands for "let go," of ourselves, to enable us to focus on the other person.

I stands for "intent," as we actively intend and are committed to listen, hear and learn.

S stands for "soak up," or absorb and understand the message that is being sent.

T stands for "transmit," our understanding of what has been said back to our child.

E stands for "echo," to check if our understanding resonates with what he intended.

N stands for "nonjudgmental," which is what we must be when we absorb the implications.

Poor Listening in Adults

The above account clearly identifies how we can improve our listening skills. Greenhalgh has grouped the signs and reasons for poor listening in adults. His three groups are "not managing oneself" listening, "getting lost in the feelings" listening and "losing the story" listening. Below is an edited description of each group, with some other comments and examples added.

"Not Managing Oneself" Listening.   This occurs when people dip in and out of listening; jump to conclusions, and then switch off; only listen when the message is one they want to hear; constantly return the conversation to their preferred topic; pretend to listen but become lost in their own thoughts; tend to compete, saying they know it, have experienced it or have thought it too; or express a judgment about what has been said, based on their own view or opinion. In other words, the listener is unwilling to "let go" of himself, as described in the LISTEN scheme above. The exchange starts and finishes with the listener who is very "self" focused.

For example:

CHILD Mom, Mr. Regan asked me to read my story to the class today.

MOM Really? That's good. That used to happen to me quite often.

CHILD It was a story about a baby being naughty in the supermarket.

MOM That's funny. I was just thinking, what would you like for dinner today?

CHILD I don't care. (Walks away, disappointed.)

A better approach would be:

CHILD   Mom, Mr. Regan asked me to read my story to the class today.

MOM   Really? It must have been good. Well done. What was it about?

CHILD   It was about a baby being naughty in the supermarket.

MOM   Ah! I bet you had fun writing that. Did it make the class laugh?

CHILD   Yes. That made me feel great.

MOM   Was there any of you in the story?

CHILD   Yup. I was the baby!

MOM   I thought as much! Has your shopping trip given you any ideas for dinner?

"Getting Lost in the Feelings" Listening. This happens when people react emotionally and impulsively to the unconscious feelings aroused in themselves; focus on the symptoms, instead of thinking more deeply about what they might mean; or think only about the feelings they usually have when they relate to the other person—which is another form of "self" focus.

For example:

CHILD   Dad, I don't want Grandpa coming to watch me play football today.

DAD   What do you mean, you don't want him to come? I can't possibly put him off. He'd be so hurt. You know how he loves to watch you. It's rude and I'm disappointed you're asking me to do that. I've talked to you before about how you speak to him!

Instead, Dad could have said:

DAD   You know that will upset him, so you must have a reason.

CHILD   Yes. You see today a talent scout is coming from the grown-ups' club to watch us. I want to do my best, and I think too many people watching me will make me nervous. Actually, I'd rather you didn't come either. Do you mind?

DAD   Of course not. I'm sure Grandpa will understand. I'll
       take him somewhere else, so he still gets an outing.
       And don't worry if you're not picked. You're doing
       well and there's plenty of time to get better.

"Losing the Story" Listening.   This happens when the listener focuses on the facts or details, instead of the whole experience, perhaps to avoid any feelings that he himself finds
hard to manage; or fails to notice surrounding nonverbal messages conveyed through body language, facial expression or
tone of voice.

For example:

MOM   (Hears a crash, a yell and rushes out to see her son in
       a heap at the bottom of the stairs) What have you
       done?
CHILD (In tears) I slipped. Can't you see?
MOM   (Offering no comfort) How many steps did you fall
       down? Were you carrying anything? What's hurting?
CHILD My foot.
MOM   Is it your toes, your ankle, your heel or what?
CHILD It just hurts.
MOM   Is it the left one or the right? Let me see it.
CHILD (Still sobbing) No, I can't move it.
MOM   I've told you so many times not to walk around in
       socks. It's asking for trouble. It can't be that bad. Try
       to get up. See if you can walk on it.

Instead, Mom could have said:

MOM   (Cuddles to give comfort) You're obviously hurt. Is the
       pain bad?
CHILD Right now, yes.
MOM   (Stays quiet with child) When you're ready, tell me
       what hurts. I'll get some ice. Poor you!

Lazy listening makes children feel ignored, misunderstood
or wrong, instead of feeling accepted, supported and encouraged. It creates a resentful and withdrawn child, and draws us

into careless talk, which makes things worse, especially for their motivation.

This book has emphasized the importance of "mastery": how we should, at every opportunity, encourage our children to be actively involved in their learning, manage things for themselves and to see and trust themselves as capable. Careless talk does the opposite; it ignores or denies a child's feelings or view of the problem. It directs a child and prevents him from sorting something out for himself. It devalues things a child sees as important. It tells him he cannot trust his judgment. In so doing, it diminishes, disempowers and demotivates him.

If we try to make a child's feelings go away, or if we disapprove of any feelings he has, he will believe he is wrong to have them. If we tell a child how to manage his feelings, he will not learn how to accept, process or take responsibility for them himself.

We should try to be more careful. Here are some examples of unhelpful and helpful ways to talk.

Ignoring a Child's Feelings or View

Challenging.   Why are you so worried about that? It's an easy problem to solve! (Can you tell me what you find difficult about these math problems?)

Reassuring.   Stop fussing. You'll have forgotten about it by tomorrow and I think you're doing just fine. (It clearly matters to you that you came in third today. Was there a special reason you wanted to do better?)

Shaming.   Don't be so sensitive. You've got to toughen up. (It's hard when our feelings are hurt.)

Minimizing.   It's really not that important. Come and have a cookie. (This seems important to you. Would you like to tell me more about it?)

Blaming. I told you you'd twist your ankle if you wore those shoes. Go and change them now. (That must have hurt. Which shoes will be comfortable for you now?)

Directing and Preventing a Child from Sorting Out for Himself

Advising. If you're so worried, go and do some more practice. That's what I'd do. (What would make you feel less worried?)

Rescuing. I'll give you an outline for your essay and then you'll have something to write about. (What's the problem? Is it the plan, your main argument or the first paragraph?)

Manipulating. You could do it that way. But really, this way is much better. Are you sure you want to do it like that? (You might like to try it your way first, and mine next time. Then you can decide which is best for you.)

Directing. Look. Do this now and then you'll have time to play on the computer later. (Make sure you plan your morning so the important things get done too. Here's some paper.)

Devaluing Things a Child Sees as Important

Excusing. You may see it as unfair, but I don't think she meant it. I wouldn't take it to heart. (I can see your point. Do you think she meant it that way, or was she under pressure?)

Dismissing. I don't know why you're so upset. It's not that big of a deal. This happens to children every day of the week. (This has upset you a lot. I can tell.)

Deflecting. Why are you so upset about not being picked as class monitor? You're great at football and will probably have the glory of being on the team. (You wanted that job badly, didn't you. Can you tell me why?)

If we are careful about what we say and how we say it, on the other hand, we can help our children.

Accepting Difficulty. Those French irregular verbs are hard to remember!

It takes a long time to get on top of all the times tables, doesn't it?

Acknowledging Feeling. You're very disappointed we're going to be away for Vijay's party, aren't you?

It's given you such a thrill to be asked to do the introduction for the school play, hasn't it!

I know there are times when you hate your brother.

Providing Encouragement to Succeed. Lots of people are anxious about learning to drive. You say you're not coordinated, but good driving is about thinking ahead, which you know you're good at.

Allowing Autonomy. "What do you think about it all now?"

"I've got myself in a mess, haven't I?"

"Mmm."

"I think I should have told my teacher about the problem a month ago."

"Yep."

"I'll go and explain it all now. It won't happen again."

FINAL TIPS ON MANAGING CONFLICT

Try not to take any dispute personally. Just because we feel it personally does not mean they meant it personally.

Show that you understand what it means to them. "You're going to be disappointed in my answer, which is no."

Keep it in proportion. It is easy to make yourself sound strong and tough by raising the stakes, but it is not helpful. "If that's your attitude, then I won't bother to cook for you anymore!" Try, instead, something like, "That's not helpful and it is not acceptable. I asked you to do this because it needs to be done. Please think again."

Try to respect things that are important to them, such as friends, how they look, what they like to do. Criticizing them creates distance that becomes ever harder to bridge.

Try not to blame them for things that have gone wrong when you are, in truth, responsible. "If you had not had your music on so loud, I wouldn't have forgotten to go to the school meeting."

Try an "opt out" tactic. Any phrase can be chosen to be used when either side feels they've gone too far and want to end the argument without losing face. When the phrase is used, the subject must be dropped instantly and not mentioned again. The tactic can be used with young children too. My daughter chose the phrase "white rabbits," and it got us off many a hook. Make sure you let your child use it first.

Remember, it usually takes six weeks to change behavior.

PART THREE

....

Rediscovering Motivation: Getting Them Back on Track

"Neither people nor problems fit moulds, and the very act of doing so can create its own problems," writes Mark H. McCormack in *What They Don't Teach You at the Harvard Business School*. Nevertheless, there are some common situations that are known to sap children's energy to do their best and undermine their motivation. If these are understood, we will be able to make our support and involvement more relevant and therefore effective. A selection of the more familiar situations is discussed in the following chapters. If none of these seems to accord with your child's experience or state of mind, the concluding chapter ends with a summary trouble-shooting guide that offers other ideas and solutions. The guide follows the stages of the motivation journey as described in Chapter 3.

17

The Impact of Stress

Motivation is affected negatively by stress, depression and uncomfortable emotions. Children who suddenly lose interest and direction in activities that previously absorbed them, or who seem to get stuck on a plateau and make no progress, may be reacting to situations and events they find hard to accept.

Contrary to common belief, stress is not something suffered only by adults. Even those who work with children can make this mistake. Usually associated with events such as divorce, unemployment, problems at work, marital disharmony and even difficult children, which happen to us only as we grow older, stress is frequently seen as a consequence of adult responsibilities: burdens that children do not have.

We also link reactions to stress, including depression, with adults. Excessive drinking, dependence on tranquilizers, staying in bed all day and, at the extreme, suicide are things we cannot conceive of young children doing. The idea that children suffer from stress and depression can seem far-fetched. If we do hear of older children abusing alcohol or drugs, we tend to see it as experimentation or rebellion. But, as Philip Graham has indicated in his booklet *So Young, So Sad, So Listen,* the reality is that rebellion itself can be a distress signal.

It can be hard to realize that a child has a problem, especially in the early stages. Like us, children have different moods, good days and bad days, go on and off people and activities and sleep better or worse for little apparent reason. However, if we ignore the early signs we can be faced with far more serious consequences later. We need to be able to recognize when both older and younger children begin to feel out of sorts.

COMMON SIGNS OF EMOTIONAL DISTRESS IN CHILDREN

Some of the most common indicators include:

- a sad, unhappy mood that lasts for more than two or three days;
- becoming withdrawn, showing little or no pleasure in ordinary, everyday activities or getting unduly immersed in television or computer games;
- different sleep patterns—waking in the night or finding it hard to go to sleep;
- appearing to be tired for no apparent reason;
- different eating and drinking patterns—stomach aches, feeling sick, losing appetite and needing more drinks to quench a stronger thirst;
- refusing or being reluctant to go to school; irritable and slow to dress in the morning and wanting to get back home again quickly after;
- bed-wetting, nail-biting, renewed thumb or finger sucking;
- becoming more uncooperative and aggressive at home and at school, including physical and verbal abuse, with both parents and siblings;
- phantom aches and pains in limbs or head and neck aches caused by tension;
- being more dependent and clingy;
- stealing, particularly when the items stolen are hoarded;
- finding concentration difficult, becoming inattentive and easily distracted;
- retreating into fantasy and make-believe, to a world where they are back in control;

- demonstrating low self-esteem, self-criticism, suicidal thoughts or behavior or striving for an inappropriate perfectionism.

Different children react differently to problems depending on their personality and age, so this list covers a wide range of behavior, even some complete opposites. Extreme behavior at either end of the range indicates distress. Most children will display one or another of these symptoms at some time. We should take special note if:

- changes in behavior are unusual and out of character;
- this behavior is inappropriate given the child's age;
- several of the above symptoms appear at the same time.

If there are grounds for concern on this basis, we can then look for a possible cause.

WHAT CHILDREN FIND DIFFICULT AND STRESSFUL

The events that cause stress and depression in adults can be hard to bear because they contain certain features that all of us, whatever our age, find difficult to manage. Knowing what these features are will give us an insight into events that can destabilize children. These features are:

- separation from those close to us—as a result of, for example, death and divorce;
- changes to our status and self-image—following marriage, birth, illness or a new job;
- changes to our routines—such as holidays, religious festivals, house and school moves.

Some of these changes are predictable and within our control; others happen without warning. Change, in itself, can be hard to cope with, but when we are caught unawares we will feel our lack of control more acutely.

Potentially stressful events, then, are those that impact our key relationships, through which we understand ourselves, and our feelings of security, by introducing change and uncertainty.

In summary, stress changes how we look at ourselves and undermines our self-esteem. It makes us feel out of control and unstable. It undermines our trust in ourselves and the future. No wonder it can stop us in our tracks.

Children, of course, do not have jobs, so cannot become unemployed. They are not responsible for family finances, so do not have money worries. They do not have husbands or wives, so cannot experience firsthand marital problems such as infidelity or sexual difficulties though, of course, they are inevitably involved when relationships break down. However, not only do children pick up on the stress and depression of adults close to them, they also have their own experiences that they find stressful, independent of family problems. They therefore get a double dose. Add to this the reality that children have less experience of life and themselves to trust that "normality" will resume, and we can see that children are more likely to be confused and disorientated by stress than adults, not less.

Looking at the three categories of stressors, we can be more attuned to the experiences children will find difficult.

Separations

Death of a Family Member.   When a child loses a parent, grandparent, brother or sister through death, many feelings are awakened. These will include fear, because someone else close might also be taken away, anger, confusion, disappointment, isolation and emptiness. Never seeing that close and treasured person again, they will miss the warmth, the support and the acceptance and identity that the now eternally absent person provided. Of course death is traumatic. Moving away from special friends can have a similar effect.

Death of a Pet.   Children are close to pets because they are warm and safe. Losing one is like losing a best friend. The death of a pet can also make children realize that parents can die too, and make them feel insecure for a while.

When Parents Split Up.   When parents decide to stop living together, most children will feel profoundly sad. They will know that something important has ended and will have a sense of loss. They will also feel shattered, and perhaps torn, because the two people who made them and have supported them are taking that support away and going in different directions.

Short- or Longer-Term Absence of a Parent.   When children are young, parents are their safety net and are always in their mind. Children depend on them for daily support. When a parent moves out, or goes away or into the hospital, even for a few days, a child can feel worried and vulnerable.

Losing or Falling Out with Friends.   Friendships become increasingly important as children grow older. Close friendships make us feel wanted and special. They help us to feel acceptable and that we belong somewhere. When a child loses a special friend, either through a school move or an argument, it will almost certainly undermine his confidence. He will feel isolated and rejected. To respond "Don't worry, you'll find another one soon" will not meet the concern or heal the hurt. Instead, we can say, "If you are lonely at break time now Vijay's decided to play with others, would it help to take a toy or game to play with?" or "It takes time to make new friends, often because others don't realize you're free to play. Is there someone you'd like to invite to dinner?"

Change in Status and Self-Image

School Changes.   When children start school, they can no longer see themselves as a baby. When they move from preschool to elementary school, or from junior high to high school, they change from being one of the oldest children in the building to being one of the youngest.

New Family Members.   The arrival of a new baby automatically changes the status of existing children, particularly the youngest. They may also have to accept new responsibilities, ready or not. At least in this case they will have a clear place in the family pecking order. Acquiring instant stepbrothers and stepsisters can produce considerable role confusion.

Illness and Hormonal Changes. Any kind of prolonged illness will change a child's self-image. Puberty involves physical changes that force children to see themselves in a different light.

Bullying. Anyone subjected to prolonged bullying will have their self-respect shattered. This subject is covered in greater depth in Chapter 20.

Work, Exam and Parental Pressures. These can turn a youngster who once felt strong and capable into someone who feels uncertain and incompetent.

Changes in Routines

Children like to know where they stand. They feel safe with routine and familiarity. It helps them to predict and to feel in control of their lives. Changes to routines can be unnerving, especially to children who already feel vulnerable. I once knew a young child whose family had two televisions. He regularly watched the black-and-white one in the family's kitchen breakfast room. The second set was a color one kept in the living room for the adults. When the kitchen was due for redecoration, he was told that he would be eating, playing and watching television in the living room for the duration. Instead of jumping with glee at the thought of watching his favorite programs in color and having access to the grown-ups' domain, he became quite disturbed and threw a tantrum. He wanted the regular television and his regular ways. This shows how a child's perspective on change can be radically different from an adult's.

ADULT STRESS IMPACTS ON CHILDREN

Family stress can be the root of children's motivation problems. Stress makes us preoccupied, withdrawn, moody and certainly less patient. We are less available and more unpredictable. We forget things, including things that our children want us to do for them, which makes them feel forgotten. Children detect changed moods and don't like it when life becomes different. They will often seek reassurance through attention-seeking behavior to receive a sign of continued love. This behavior is usually "difficult," otherwise it will not have the desired effect. It can easily be misinterpreted and lead, instead, to more apparent rejection. Very young children will simply behave badly; older children may stop working or go out more. They may change their eating habits or style of dress. If, after trying several times, they don't get the reassurance they seek, they will try to protect themselves by cutting off.

HOW MANY CHILDREN ARE AFFECTED BY STRESS?

No one can be absolutely sure, partly because it is difficult to agree on definitions in a field concerned with states of mind and partly because children can suffer without anyone knowing. Nonetheless, there is wide agreement among those working in this area that mental health problems are relatively common in children and young people. Young Minds, the U.K. children's mental health charity, estimates that up to 20 percent may require help at some time. This amounts to nearly 2 million children under the age of sixteen in England and Wales. Seven to 10 percent of all children have problems that are moderate to severe, and as many as 2 percent suffer from severe mental health problems. Dr. Stephen Scott, consultant child psychiatrist at the Institute of Psychiatry at the Maudsley Hospital in London, suggests that about 10 percent of children have problems that are significantly disabling. For Scott, these are problems that "stop children and adolescents doing the normal things, being able to make friends, go to school, function productively . . . persistent problems lasting for a year or more which really handicap the ability to be happy."

There is mounting evidence to suggest that problems at the severe end are growing. Eating disorders are on the increase among younger children. Attempted suicides and deliberate self-harm are all on the increase. Around 2 in 100 children are seriously depressed, and the number of children and young people admitted as psychiatric in-patients in hospitals is growing.

It would be safe to say that any statistics represent the tip of the iceberg. For each of these cases, there will be many more where young people came close to not coping but were able to hold on to normality. These statistics also relate mostly to older children whose problems will almost certainly have taken root much earlier.

HOW STRESS DISRUPTS MOTIVATION

We all have a point beyond which pressure and challenge stop being exciting and manageable, and we crack. The more we have to manage, the less we are able to cope. Like weights added to one side of those old-fashioned, seesaw scales, it can be an apparently insignificant issue, the smallest weight, that upsets the balance and tips us over into feelings of failure and panic. At this point, even normal tasks seem difficult. We lose confidence and we lose self-belief. We lose energy and can become intensely preoccupied with our problems and failures.

A child cannot learn unless he feels at ease with himself. This means that unpleasant emotions have to be faced and managed. Only then can he relax comfortably and concentrate. Most parents are able to understand that if a child is preoccupied with a problem and feels swamped with the emotions it brings in its train, he will not be able to clear his thoughts sufficiently to focus on anything else. But this is only part of the picture.

Fear—of failure, success or the unknown—prevents children from opening up and trying. Anxiety keeps children in suspension, and makes them unwilling to commit to answers, opinions or actions. Anger makes children boil; it takes them over. Jealousy can be the spur to outdo someone else but it can also preoccupy a child. Resentment makes children uncooperative, cut themselves off and want revenge on those who have hurt them. Hatred causes children to withdraw cooperation. Children can hate because they feel let down, because their trust has been abused or they feel used. Hostility is closely linked to depression.

Emotions and Self-Esteem

These feelings occur in situations that are likely to damage a child's self-esteem, which adds a further twist to the dynamic of underachievement. If we hate, it is because someone has been unpleasant to us and we might believe we deserved that treatment. If we are jealous, it is because we fear that another person is liked better than ourselves. If we are envious, we covet something that somebody else has and feel incomplete without it. Resentment grows when we feel someone has ignored our interests or exploited us. Anxiety relates to a belief that we can't, or won't be able to, cope. We don't feel in charge and our competence is threatened. If we are angry, it is usually because we are frustrated and feel powerless. Yet motivation requires inner strength and good self-belief. It is not just strong, negative emotions that interfere with motivation but also the situations that give rise to them.

GETTING THEM BACK ON TRACK

We can support children through their difficulties. We can try to listen to what children say, and be sensitive to their behavior. If they:

- raise something important, wherever possible we should stop what we are doing and give them our full attention;
- behave out of character, we should try to attune ourselves to their needs by watching and interpreting their behavior;
- stop talking and listening to us, it may be because things are too strained. In these cases, it can be helpful to enlist another adult who knows our child well and suggest that he or she create an opportunity to talk.

Encourage Children to Talk

It can be hard to start a discussion about sensitive matters, especially with older children who may be defensive. Instigating a conversation at the appropriate moment, saying something like "You don't seem to have been yourself recently. I don't like to see you so down. I just want to let you know that I am here for you whenever you want to talk," lets them know we are aware and concerned but hands the initiative to them.

If you want to try to get children to talk, choose a quiet place when there is plenty of time. With a younger child, it can help to look at a children's storybook that covers the same or similar situation and feelings he is experiencing. With an older child, spending more open-ended time together may create a moment when he feels able to take the initiative. One teenage boy of divorced parents I met told me his father used to ask him how he felt about the divorce when driving him home after weekend visits. It was a short journey, and the son felt insulted not only because the time available was so limited but also because it came across as a convenient "quick fix" that demonstrated little genuine concern.

Acknowledge and Accept Feelings

Let them know we realize they are feeling something that is normal and understandable. Telling them they have no reason to feel that way will not reassure them. Encourage children to express their feelings in acceptable ways—through painting, drawing, music, imaginative play sport or creative design, especially if they are too young to talk or are finding it hard.

Take away any guilt they might feel. When things go wrong in families, even when someone dies, children can feel it is their fault. We can help to remove any self-recrimination they feel if we can explain clearly that they are not responsible or to blame in any way.

Help Them Feel Secure

Keeping as many routines going as possible through any changes will provide some continuity, security and comfort to offset any difficulties. Any other changes that are not essential are best kept to a minimum.

It can help our children if we actually tell them we love them and if we try to be around a bit more.

Boost Their Self-Esteem and Self-Belief

Show them that you accept and love them for who they are. Try to understand them and their feelings. Give them plenty of time and attention. Children who are depressed or not doing well at anything could be feeling insignificant. Talking and doing things together and being around more will help them to trust your love, feel wanted and therefore feel better and cope more easily.

Create some "motivation momentum" by letting them know you think they are good at things. Avoid criticism. Give them chances to try new activities so they can discover new talents.

If they have few friends and don't go out much, try to encourage them to be more sociable. Joining a club or an activity group can open up social opportunities, though older children may refuse this point blank.

Attention-seeking behavior is attention-needing behavior. Don't let bad behavior be the only way to get attention.

Keep Them Informed

Tell them what is happening as far as possible. They will know something is different, and they will be able to understand it at their level. Try to answer their questions honestly and take their worries seriously.

If there are family disputes, we should try not to confide in our children, ask them to take sides or require them to keep secrets. The responsibility and divided loyalty this causes is very hard for children to manage.

Offering them some choices about events surrounding the happening, provided these are appropriate, can help children to feel respected and included, not left out and ignored.

Look After Yourself

Children who are feeling insecure need much more attention, but it is usually only possible to give this if you feel strong and confident yourself. Where difficulties stem from home, it is very likely that you will also be feeling vulnerable. Looking after yourself will help you to help your child.

Think about what helps you to calm down, relax and feel better. Build it in to your day or week. Reduce the pressures on yourself. Drop unnecessary chores when you can. Tasks seem less overpowering if you list them in order of importance. Make it clear to the family what you need. You are entitled to have some time alone, for example, provided it still leaves room for them.

Listen and talk more. Understanding how each person sees the problem is the first step to sorting things out—so talking and listening to others in your family helps. So does sharing problems with friends.

It really does not help to feel guilty. And it will certainly add insult to injury if we pass on that guilt in the form of blame, making it appear as if they are responsible. Raise your own self-esteem by listing your good points and your successes. Do this with a friend if it will help.

18

Peer Pressure: Friends or Foes?

Friends are important to children, whatever their age. When your child's friends "fit" your family, it gives you a lovely feeling. Not only do you feel warm, proud and relieved that your child is accepted by others as a whole human being and is able to be a friend to others, you are also grateful that your family boat is not being rocked by unwelcome influences. When you don't have to worry, friends are great to have around. The situation is far less rosy when children "get in with the wrong crowd," when friends subvert your plans, challenge your values and cause problems.

Peer pressure is almost always understood negatively. We use the term when our children want us to buy the "right" kind of clothes and shoes that usually cost more than we want to pay. We use it when we are pressed to acquire the latest craze toy, when we know it will be a passing fad and forgotten as quickly as it was grabbed. We use it when our children are persuaded to behave disruptively at school and take their eye off the learning ball. And we use it when we are bludgeoned with requests to allow later bedtimes or homecoming times, trips to raves or visits to rock concerts. The tensions caused by peer pressure can, then, start early, despite being commonly associated with the teenage years. To add to parents' frustration, peer pressure usually comes well laced with values different from our own.

If we are to have any success in encouraging our children to achieve a different balance in their lives, to stay true to themselves rather than be lured and diverted by the call of others, we need to understand why peer pressure can be so hard to resist.

WHY FRIENDS ARE IMPORTANT

Children like to have friends. With friends, they feel they belong, they feel liked and likeable. Friends validate them, and match their current needs and interests. They help to define who they are, giving them an identity. "I am friends with this sort of person so I am also like this." Friends help them to fill their time and have fun, to become sociable and learn to be part of a group. They give them confidence to do things they would be reluctant to do on their own—both desirable and less desirable—and they provide safety in numbers. Friends can offer new ideas and interests, adding to experience, and can provide a relevant, moral framework. Real friends will offer support and care, volunteer loyalty and provide a safe haven when things go wrong. Friends become, quite simply, part of themselves, which makes it very hard for us to persuade them to change course.

Friends can be "satisfying and growth-producing," or they can be the cause of distress and be "growth-destroying," to quote Mary Pipher in her book, *Reviving Ophelia*, on adolescent girls. Peers are not the same thing as friends. Not all peers are friends, and not all friends are peers, though they usually are. Children themselves can get confused between the two. It is a useful distinction for parents to bear in mind, as we shall see shortly. Peers are all those of a similar age who share their world—geographical, educational and social. The peer group will be broader than a friendship group, and influenced by more widespread values. Friends can be single or grouped. Though influenced by peer values, friendship groups will usually have more specific interests and attitudes in common.

ARE THEY REALLY FOES?

Parents can become almost tribal in their defensive reactions to the changes that the outside world foists on their children. I remember very clearly my daughter coming home from primary school not just with a different way of talking picked up from the playground, but also with clothes smelling different—a mixture of school dinners and disinfectant. I did not like it. I wondered if she was going to stay like that. In the same way, friends who introduce "foreign" values can be difficult to accept. However we do need to try to keep things in perspective. Conflict over friends is likely to drive children away and reduce our influence still further, so it is important to keep our views and interventions for those times when it really matters. Here are some factors we can consider if we think our child's friends are exerting a bad influence.

First, our children may be entering a time of change. They have to experiment with their developing selves, and it is common for them to try themselves out with different friendship groups. They were going to change anyway. Trust them to settle with friends who reflect their earlier family experiences—or let them be different if they are not at the same time jeopardizing their future opportunities.

Second, it is inevitable that our children will live their lives differently from how we lived ours as children. It may seem threatening, and we may regret lost innocence, but this is the world they live in.

Third, a wider variety of experiences, handled responsibly and within clear limits, will prepare them well for a future full of choices and temptations.

Fourth, as children grow, they need to get into mischief, make mistakes and pay the price for these. In general, we are far more aware of what our children get up to these days. Worry about alcohol, drugs and crime can encourage us to overreact and become overprotective.

So when should we start to worry? Some children do go seriously off course. Whether this is directly and solely the responsibility of their friends is something we have to ask ourselves. Sometimes, it is wise to start looking closer to home; work, first and foremost, on giving them a strong, positive identity that they can feel proud of and that will help them to stay resistant and safe.

Children's sense of self, their self-esteem, is tightly bound up in their friendships. The stronger their sense of who they are, the less they will get seduced by the pull of an unhelpful peer group. The more they learn to trust their own judgment, and can practice saying "No," the more likely they are to recognize trouble in the making and have the confidence to walk away. The more they see themselves as unwanted, feel a failure or find it hard to please, the more they will seek status in alternative, and possibly illegitimate, ways.

We often hear about friends who think it is not "cool" to study, but occasionally peer pressure encourages children to strive too hard. The tide of competition can drive children to try to achieve an undue perfection, typically exhibiting eating problems along with it.

If we feel the need to redirect our child, it is tricky to achieve this without undermining him, showing insensitivity to his needs and damaging his trust in his judgments. Whatever tactics we choose, we should ensure that they preserve his self-respect and protect his self-belief and self-esteem.

GETTING THEM BACK ON TRACK

As children choose friends to meet various needs listed above, try to make a list of the things your child may be getting from the group he is currently friends with. Can any of these needs be met in other ways? Try to talk to him about what he expects from a friend. Respect for his point of view, reliability, the ability to understand and compromise might be features raised. It will be up to him, then, to consider if his current "friends" are really people who deserve his loyalty. It is dangerous for you to say they are no good.

If you feel that work or other, genuine, interests are getting crowded out by the temptations of new friends, perhaps you could discuss together what his various commitments and interests are and seek ways to meet them all. Speaking to the other parents involved to consider the scope for a shared set of rules and expectations may help. Consider if there are any clubs to join or new sporting or other activities to take up to widen the circle of friends available.

Acknowledge and welcome the changes that come with growing up so he can be proud of these, but suggest that we always move forward with some of our old self still in place. We are like snakes, shedding a skin but with our existing body intact. Which bit of his old self is still there, that he can still explore to maintain continuity and stay in touch with himself?

Explain that he does not have to sell his soul to be popular. He can want to be liked, at the same time as be unwilling to make the compromises necessary. It is strong, not weak, to stand up against negative things, such as treating other people badly or breaking the law, that the group likes to do. Make sure he knows it is okay to say "No" when something is really important to him, and that it is okay to make mistakes.

Allow him to redefine himself in an accepting atmosphere. Try to reduce the amount of teasing, carping and criticism. Be as encouraging, supportive and nonjudgmental as possible. Try to keep your worries to yourself. Predicting academic, sporting or social failure will only undermine his self-belief, and it could drive him away. Accept and love him for who he is. Give him space, responsibility and the chance to be useful to you so he can find out more about what he can do. Try to compromise more to avoid too many clashes, but hold firm on a few important issues to you so you retain some authority and respect.

If you have room at home, invite his friends over, so you appear to accept them and can learn more about them than first impressions allow. Also spend more time together as a family, and include a friend or two from time to time if that is possible. Consider whether any of your friends have children of a suitable age, and if so, invite them all over.

Try to speak optimistically about the future and his role in it, to give him hope. Encourage him to mix with other age groups if possible, perhaps within the family, so he gets another perspective on life and relationships. At the same time keep yourself in touch with his world, without currying favor, aping it or taking it over. Read his magazines, be prepared to listen to his music, talk to other parents, show interest in his school and out-of-school interests. Try to have some meals together so you can chat about his view of things.

And remember: friends can work as well as play together. They can offer mutual support and motivation.

19

The Dejected Child—
"I'm Just Useless!"

Most children will go through times when they feel out of their depth. This is natural, because learning is a constant process of pushing against the frontiers of knowledge. There are new skills to learn and longer time frames to manage. Some children sail through, but not many. Children who have no problems making progress in one aspect of learning may have difficulties elsewhere. Some children surge forward in every sphere for a while, and then find things hardgoing. Learning is not linear; it takes place in fits and starts. But when problems loom, they can loom large. Self-judgment can become punitive. When children are really low, they will feel useless all around. They will tear up or deface work that they believe is not good enough, and they may have difficulty completing projects, giving up before they have really tried. Success elsewhere, or at other times, will make little impact—"That doesn't count," will be a typical response when they are reminded. This is because what we are good at we find easy; and when it is easy, we find it hard to value any success in that sphere as an achievement.

WHY MIGHT THEY BE FEELING THIS WAY?

As was noted in Chapter 3, children can get lost at different stages on the motivation journey. They can be confronted with, or choose, an inappropriate target at stage one. They can fail to assess their skill level sensibly, and fall by the wayside at stage two. They can jump in the deep end, forgetting the need to plan their approach to the target at stage three. They can wilt under the strain of boredom or setbacks at stage four, and find it hard to sustain the commitment necessary. Or they can simply be too hard on themselves, having standards that are too high, which prevents them from recognizing when they have done well and arrived at stage five.

The root of the problem can lie deeper, in self-doubt, in which case we have to ask why they feel this way. It can be linked to:

- the drip, drip effect of negative labeling from others, including us, telling them they are "useless," "a loser," "a hopeless case" or "a dumbo";

- the fact that they tried extra hard this time, and it still made no difference;

- someone saying something careless, such as "You had your chance and you blew it" or "How long is it going to take you to get this right?";

- comparing themselves with a more able child;

- realizing that, however hard they try, they will never be as good as a particular person they admire or are competing against;

- something that has happened in their wider life to affect their powers of concentration, memory and listening so they not only start to fall behind but also feel insecure;

- their personality—they are that sort of child, but beware that explanation; children are not born incompetent.

WATCH WHAT YOU SAY

When children are vulnerable, you have to be particularly careful how you respond. What you say has to be real—there is no point saying that something is wonderful when clearly it is not—and sound acceptable to them. You have to find the way through their heightened sensitivity to criticism. The danger is that their self-denigration will make you feel impotent and frustrated and more likely to respond insensitively.

What We Tend to Say

We are easily tempted into offering instant solutions that minimize the problem because, as we saw in Chapter 16, many parents consider they have neither the time nor the emotional energy to manage such intangible problems. We would prefer to wave a magic wand and make it all better. That way, we can also avoid feeling our child's pain and despair. At the harsh end of typical responses are, "You're not the best, but you're not that bad either. Stop feeling sorry for yourself and just get on with it" or "If you only listened in class, perhaps you'd understand it." Less critical, but equally directive and unsupportive, are comments such as "You're not useless. You came in third last week. I don't want to hear you put yourself down," "You'll feel completely different next week" or "What's wrong with a B+?" In each of these cases, the child's feelings are being denied. This will simply convey to a child that there is something wrong with him if he feels this way. It will not help him to rediscover his confidence and courage.

Chapter 16 also looked at how parents and other adults can respond carelessly to children's feelings and anxieties, denying, excusing, dismissing them. The guidance given there applies especially to the dejected child.

What We Should Try to Say

Dejected children need, instead, careful talk. We have to use language that is wholly encouraging and untainted with judgment or qualification. We must avoid the mixed messages typical of backhanded compliments ("You did pretty well, given your slow start"), references to past failures ("You played that beautifully this time, but why couldn't you play like that last week?") or requests for further improvement ("If you train even harder, you could come in first"). As we have already seen, there are a number of components to careful talk that must be adhered to.

First, we should listen, attentively and effectively, to what our child has to say, without interruption. We can then accept the problem as he sees it, and acknowledge his feelings. When it comes to discussing what might be done to improve things, we can ask, not tell, and allow him to come to his own conclusions. Instead of offering advice, we can ask relevant questions. "What do you think brought it about?" "How long have you been feeling like this?" or "Do you have any ideas about what would make it easier for you?" Finally, we can leave the door open for further discussion. This shows him that we are there for him when he needs it. "If you get low again, remember that I am here to listen whenever you want."

WHEN PRAISE DOES NOT WORK

When children are very low, they often reject praise, the first thing we do to help. First, it will take time for them to accept any view of themselves that is different from their own. Second, they will be very sensitive to sincerity and intention. If they feel manipulated by the praise, they will ignore it. If they feel judged, they may trust their own judgment more than a parent's or teacher's. If they are encouraged to try again, or harder, without addressing the source of their anxiety, they may feel they are simply exposing themselves to more failure. Hanko and Hall both state, from their different standpoints of education and sports, that we need to start from the child's anxiety, the underlying feelings and reasons for it, and allow the child to take himself forward, at his own pace. He has to feel in control. As Hanko writes, by finding out from a child how he views a problem ("Do I know what this task is about?" "Do I know how to go about it?" "Am I able to complete it?"), we can then encourage him to assess his own progress ("How are you getting on?" "Is it as hard as you thought?" "What were the difficult bits?" "Why do you think you did so well?").

Dejected and discouraged children need help to rediscover their capable selves and to see new possibilities. Although their problem is their own, not ours—they have to reframe and redefine themselves, to their satisfaction, and only they can reinflate their self-belief—parents can be an important source of strength to children during such times.

We should accept our child for who he is, which includes his fears, anxieties, strengths and vulnerabilities, by listening, and giving time and attention. We can keep all criticisms and judgments to a minimum, especially in relation to those skills our child feels he lacks. We must listen to, understand, accept and validate his feelings, and avoid belittling, denying or ridiculing these, even if we feel frustrated or irritated by them, or feel inadequate because we believe our child is incompetent and unconfident. If we reflect back to our child his feelings of inadequacy, it will help him to feel understood. It does not mean we agree with him.

We must give him experience of success by giving plenty of praise, lowering our sights and expectations and valuing a range of different talents. If we reduce the risk in what he does by giving clearer instructions, making things slightly easier for a time or by just letting him rest for a while in the comfort of what he can manage, this will help. Appreciation of anything he has done that we like, such as cleaning up after himself, will boost his self-belief.

Our child will need help to assess himself in a less negative way. In response to cries of "I'm just useless," we can say: "Hang on a moment. Let's just sit down and list those things you are good at. Don't write yourself off just because one or two things aren't going well at the moment!" "How bad was it, really? Did everybody else do brilliantly and you were the only one who flunked?" or "Take it step by step. What is the first thing you think you need to do to turn things around? If you can't answer that now, come back in fifteen minutes and tell me."

If we help him to judge how much of a problem he has, using a technique explained by Hall, we can help our child reassess his competence. Draw a line, and explain that the left-hand end of the line represents knowing nothing, while the right-hand end represents knowing everything. Then invite your child to mark the place on the line where he thinks he falls. Although he will exclaim in absolutes ("I don't know anything!"), when pushed to represent how much he knows he will be more realistic.

We can encourage him to identify things he is good at. Remember, such attributes as social skills, sporting skills, kindness to others and knowledge of natural history all count. This will help to put him in touch, in Hanko's words, with his "untapped or negated resources."

A child has to be in charge of something if he is to feel capable. If we give him plenty of useful, practical things to do to help us and others, he will feel depended on and therefore dependable.

Positive thinking is essential, so we must model more positive self thoughts. If we constantly put ourselves down, this becomes a pattern that our child will copy.

20

Good Times, Bad Times: Problems at School

School is a major part of a child's life. When things go wrong at school, through bullying, work pressure or personality differences with the teacher, the problems cannot be parceled up and forgotten. They invade, intrude and impede children's thoughts, feelings and actions at night and during the day, when working, resting or playing. We must take these problems seriously, both to prevent them from getting worse and to protect our child's self-esteem, which, if damaged, could begin a downward spiral of underachievement, friendship difficulties and more permanent demotivation.

BULLYING AND FRIENDSHIP PROBLEMS

Social and relationship difficulties at school cover a wide range of problems. They include being isolated and alone, ignored rather than included, pestered by a clinging friend, teasing, name-calling, being kept out of games or being jostled, and more serious taunting, destruction of belongings, extortion and physical and verbal aggression. Bullying is deliberate, sustained behavior that is intended to frighten or hurt. It is usually done by one particular individual, or by a group organized by a particular person.

Where a child is victimized and intimidated for a long period, the result can be devastating. Even milder forms of teasing and taunting will force children to question themselves. Their self-belief will be, at the very least, dented. Only the strongest will continue to value themselves to the same degree as before in the face of such prolonged hostility. Serious bullying can destroy self-respect, lead to serious depression and, rarely, suicide. It would be very surprising if any child could remain on task and motivated during the dark days of self-doubt resulting from humiliation, isolation and rejection at the hands of others.

If your child suddenly loses direction, and bullying—mild or severe—is the reason, it is important to act swiftly. This may be difficult. Parents are often the last to know, because children can find it hard to talk about their troubles and own up to what they see as their personal weakness. There are telltale signs to look out for. The list of symptoms of stress in children in Chapter 17 is a useful starting point. Look out particularly for any change in behavior and attitudes in relation to school. Your child might be withdrawn in the mornings and reluctant to get ready to go, shed tears or have disturbed sleep at night or suddenly lose confidence in his work and himself. Any of these events will indicate the time is right to talk and discuss with him ways that will bring it to an end.

GETTING THEM BACK ON TRACK

Put your child's mind at rest. Reassure him that it is not his fault, that there's nothing wrong with him and nothing to be ashamed of. Listen attentively to what your child says takes place, and believe it. Tell the school, and talk to other parents about their children's experiences.

Talk to your child about useful strategies. Teach him games you played as a child, and together discuss phrases he will feel comfortable using that will make him sound and feel stronger. "Would you like to play with me?" is stronger than "Can I play with you?" and "That looks like a good game. Can you teach it to me?" sounds better than "Can I play too?" Saying something like "Bullies are weak. I think I know why you need to do this" or "I don't like it when you pull my jacket," before walking confidently away, is assertive; withdrawing, looking hurt, shows the bullies they have won.

According to the reports of some adults who were bullied as children, hitting or hurting back sometimes works. It calls the bully's bluff. Nevertheless, physical violence is not something that parents should recommend. First, it teaches that violence is the right way to solve even minor problems, which it is not. Second, any response not made confidently and convincingly will be ineffective and is liable to make matters worse.

Suggest that he make a friend of anyone else on his own, as children in groups are less likely to be picked on. Also, help your child to compromise, problem-solve and take turns at home to reduce potential clashes at school.

If possible, involve him in children's groups outside school so he can lose the "victim" label and regain social confidence.

More generally, try making him feel loved and accepted. Help to build his confidence by letting him know he is good at things, and give him lots of praise and encouragement.

EXAM AND WORK PRESSURES

Work and exam pressure can become intolerable and intensely stressful for children of any age. ChildLine, the children's telephone help line, has produced a pamphlet called *Stressed Out: What Children Tell ChildLine About Exams and Work Pressure*. It reports findings from a survey of children in school and the telephone calls it receives. Many older children feel that their whole future hangs in the balance at times of key examinations. "They described feeling out of control, panic-stricken, overburdened and overwhelmed, often saying they could not cope any more and, occasionally, they were suicidal. Many said they had little support and that they felt unable to confide in those around them." In their own words: "Everyone expects too much of me." "I'm just stupid and abnormal."

"Mom and Dad just don't realize I'm not as clever as my brother." "I feel stuck, as if there's no way out." "I feel like I am in a box, shouting at them to listen."

So much depends now not simply on passing exams but on passing well enough to gain a competitive edge. Schools are even adding to the self- and parent-imposed pressure. League tables, parental choice and the way the size of school budgets is calculated mean that each school has a vested interest in their students' performance, even at age seven. Their future depends on it. Children feel they are under a spotlight that is becoming laser-intense.

It was reported in a newspaper recently that the South Korean government is going to convict and imprison parents who put too much pressure on their children. New legislation aims to stop what is described as "academic slavery," following a spawning of private cramming schools, which two-thirds of the country's children attend after daytime school from primary age upward. "My school life," reported an eighteen-year-old who is forced by his parents to study from 7:30 A.M. until midnight, "is a constant battle against sleep."

We have not gone that far, but some children suffer intensely from the pressure their parents place on them. One fifteen-year-old ChildLine caller was studying for nine exams and also had a part-time job. Her mother had very high expectations of her, demanding straight A's. The girl was threatened with having to leave home if she failed to get the grades necessary for her to follow her chosen course. She was very distressed and finding it hard to eat.

GETTING THEM BACK ON TRACK

Try to be sensitive to the early signs of problems. The more stressed children are, the more they need to feel secure emotionally. Try to make them feel important to you, and keep family conflict, with them or with others, to a minimum. Let them know you accept them for who they are, not what they can do. They must work for themselves, not to please you.

Give them support, by getting them drinks and snacks while they work, by listening, by asking them if they are finding anything difficult, by finding a family friend or neighbor who may know more about something they are stuck on. Help them to plan their revision or studying. Breaking the task down into bite-size chunks makes work more manageable. Remember the 80:20 rule—working 80 percent harder to do 20 percent better is not an efficient use of time.

Let them study in the way that suits them best. Each child is different: some like to work late at night; others like to get up early. Some prefer to work in short bursts; others like working for longer stretches before then taking a complete break. Social life or part-time jobs may be compatible with their work commitments so let them decide, after discussion with you, if possible. Try to trust their ability to do well without pressure from you. Pressure demonstrates lack of trust; it is a form of power. And what are the two rules of misused power? The more you use it, the more you lose it; and you bring about that which you fear.

If you think you may be asking for a lot, try to reassess your expectations. Ask yourself what is really important and realize that there are many different ways children can lead fulfilled and happy lives.

PERSONALITY CLASHES— "MY TEACHER DOESN'T LIKE ME!"

Children often lose interest in a subject or activity because of personality differences with the teacher—either they do not like the teacher or they believe their teacher does not like them. The two are often linked. Either way, children rarely pull out the stops for a teacher they don't feel comfortable with.

Few teachers will say to a child's face that he is disliked. If your child believes it to be true, it is his interpretation. It might be true, because teachers, like the rest of us, find it hard to hide their real feelings, and children are canny creatures; but it might not be true. Just because a teacher shows, perhaps, a passing irritation does not necessarily mean general dislike.

Of course, some teaching styles and personalities work well with certain types of learners and not well with others. However, it is worthwhile exploring with your child what, specifically, has made him decide he is not liked. Perhaps he feels picked on.

TALKING TO THE TEACHER

When a child is unhappy, for whatever reason, his work, friendships and behavior can suffer. It therefore helps to tell someone at school, or anyone else who works closely with him.

Even when we accept that telling someone may help, it is never easy to decide when, where and how to do it. It often takes particular courage to approach the school, especially if we think the school is at fault. There are several reasons for this. We might expect that somehow, we'll get blamed. We might feel what we say will be kept in a file and be held against us or our child. We might prefer to keep this information private, wishing it were none of the school's business. We might fear being labeled pushy—or overprotective, or short-tempered. Even parents who are teachers can find themselves turning to jelly when reaching for the telephone or walking up the hall. There are ways to make communication easier.

To achieve a comfortable, nonconfrontational meeting, remember to do the following:

- Make an appointment. It's not advisable to go in when you are feeling very upset about something.

- Say what your concern is when the appointment is made. For example, "It's a personal matter" or "My son's not happy at the moment and I want to talk about why."

- Prepare yourself. Think ahead about how something is best said.

- Prioritize what you want to discuss and deal with the most important point first. Don't start with the least important one just because it seems "safe," otherwise the matter you have really come for might get forgotten. Think twice about listing all your points in an introduction, especially those that may seem confrontational, as this may put the teacher on the defensive.

- Avoid getting sidetracked. Have a written list of things you want to raise and don't be afraid to refer to it.
- Avoid the appearance of telling teachers what to do by explaining what has worked at home. "Tom seems happier to read when he sees he can manage the first page" is better than "The books you give him to bring home are discouraging him from reading."
- Translate any complaint or verbal attack from the teacher into a worry: "It sounds as if you are worried that Ben won't. . ."

It is important to remember that our child's health, happiness and future should come first, above any personal discomfort and embarrassment. The child should be the school's priority too. Having the same aim should help both sides to problem-solve together. We should certainly expect information to be exchanged, in a two-way process. This is what home-school partnership means.

It is usually better to approach the classroom teacher first, and only take it to the head teacher or principal if you do not get satisfaction. Always bear in mind that you are the expert on your child, and that you have a right to be concerned and to discuss any worries you have.

When you go in, think carefully about whether you tell your child. Sometimes it is better to keep it to yourself. More often, though, children value being told the truth and given a chance to influence what you are going to say. This makes them feel involved, not worried or suspicious.

21

The Gifted Child

Gifted children and their parents are usually considered extremely lucky. The very term "gifted" implies this. If the talent is seen as a gift, it must be desirable. The child can feel proud of himself. The parent does not have to worry about whether his or her child succeeds. People may be surprised, then, to discover a chapter devoted to gifted children in a book on motivation, and especially to find it in a section dealing with problems.

Yet educational, social, behavioral and emotional problems are quite frequent among gifted children—at least until their ability is recognized and responded to. Why? And if highly able children experience problems with underachievement and poor motivation, where might this stem from and what can parents do to help them get back on track?

CHARACTERISTICS OF GIFTED AND ABLE CHILDREN

These questions are easier to answer if we understand something about what very able and gifted children can be like. Sometimes, the very characteristics they have as gifted children—the way they are—can provoke others to respond and react in ways that undermine the child, causing him to feel misunderstood and dejected.

What are these characteristics? Perhaps frustratingly, there is no agreed upon, simple definition for high ability or giftedness. There is wide agreement, though, about the sort of abilities and ways of thinking and doing things that set these children apart. Very able children probably constitute about 5 percent of the child population, and the term "exceptionally able" is usually taken to refer to the smaller number, about 2 percent, who are capable of functioning at a level several years in advance of what is considered normal for their age group.

In the United States, educationalists use different versions of a similar typology, which describes the difference between a bright child and a very able or gifted learner. It is useful for highlighting the relevant characteristics that can cause problems. An example of this typology is selectively reproduced below.

Bright Child	Gifted Child
Knows the answer	Asks questions
Is interested	Is highly curious
Is attentive	Is involved
Has good ideas	Has wild, "silly" ideas
Reads and writes well	Enjoys the use of language, especially its use in humor
Learns with ease	Often looks for hidden difficulties
Listens with interest	Shows strong feelings and opinions
6–8 repetitions for mastery	1–2 repetitions for mastery
Understands ideas	Constructs abstractions
Well-presented work	Messy presentation because thoughts are rushing ahead
Enjoys peers	Often prefers adults
Absorbs information	Manipulates information

Gifted children can become demotivated because they:

- are inadequately challenged;
- are put down for being themselves—exposing their talents and knowledge;
- wish to conform—underperforming so they can appear "normal";
- feel frustrated because their ideas are ahead of their ability to carry them out.

Verbal Fluency

From the list of characteristics above, it can be seen that gifted children will often be very good with words, which means that they will talk fluently and at length, but their written work will not always be up to the same standard. Schools naturally look at the quality and the speed of written work for "proof" of a child's exceptional ability. Frustration, boredom and learning to fill the time available with extraneous thoughts can lead these children to work slowly, so the "proof" is not forthcoming.

Verbal fluency also means a gifted child may prefer to talk to an adult than to a classmate, someone who is more likely to comprehend his latest schemes and ideas. Desperate for a soul mate, he can easily come across as irritating, and his pestering may be interpreted as an attempt to curry favor and brag.

Quick to Understand

The gifted child will be a quick learner, who does not need to practice much, if at all, in order to understand new concepts. Repeating tasks will be boring, and may even lead to careless mistakes, which many adults will read as proof that more work or practice is necessary. If a child takes the initiative to move his own learning forward, or shows that he already knows the next stage, he can easily be reprimanded for being arrogant or for stepping out of line.

Curiosity and Humor

Gifted children can be creative and abstract thinkers with a pronounced curiosity and an unstoppable sense of humor. Always asking questions, always wanting to take the discussion and explanation further, offering wild and apparently silly ideas and frequently cracking verbal jokes, it is easy to see how the constant disruption to carefully constructed explanations would interrupt the concentration of the class and be disapproved of. Being strong on imagination and the ability to concentrate, gifted children are inclined to become frustrated without a real challenge and to pursue other, more absorbing thoughts. Yet the problem is usually defined as an inability to concentrate.

Know-It-Alls

Very able children may come across as irritating know-it-alls because they often have a good memory, wide general knowledge and surprisingly deep understanding and excitement about some particular field of interest that they want to share. Where their wide knowledge is combined with a tendency to express strong feelings and opinions and an enjoyment of logical argument, their assertiveness can be perceived as verging on the insufferable.

HOW IT MIGHT FEEL TO BE DIFFERENT

There is a saying in Japan, where conformity is highly valued, that if a nail sticks up, hammer it back in. Although British and American education has been renowned for its encouragement of individuality and creativity, the classroom reality is all too often that excellence is frowned upon. You can be a personality, but you cannot outshine anyone else. Many gifted children will find themselves being hammered back in, either by their teachers, who should know better, or by their class-mates who can feel threatened by someone who is more capable, or just "different." Sometimes, very able children will stamp on themselves, in effect hammering themselves back in, to stay "normal" so they do not stand out.

Given all the above, how might a gifted child feel? He may feel put down, even punished, for being himself. He may feel disliked and see himself as a nuisance. He will also feel profound frustration and disappointment that he has been misjudged and misunderstood, and be confused about whether it is okay to be the person that he feels he is. He will often be made to feel different, as strange and freakish rather than special, though it may not be intended. He may therefore feel quite isolated, cut off from the other children around him: not quite a child but in a child's body. In these circumstances it will be hard to stay comfortable with himself.

If he decides to conform, either to please adults or to get closer to his peers, he will be unable to relax. He must manipulate what he thinks and says constantly to ensure that he does not show himself up. He has to underachieve, and in so doing loses touch with himself. He may even forget what he can do, and spontaneity disappears. He can never experience any pride in an achievement, unless he produces different quality work in the privacy of his home, which is what many such children do—for their own self-respect.

Gifted children will also find it hard to be true to themselves in two further ways. The first is that their enthusiasm, depth of understanding and ideas will often encourage them to set targets for themselves that are simply not attainable without great application or adult support. Plans for projects or ideas for stories are not so much grandiose as overambitious for the child that they are. Usually reading at an advanced level, this is the prose they hear in their heads but cannot always put into words—let alone actually write on paper. Yet they desperately want to write—a book, an in-depth school project or similar ambitious scheme. For those who want to do rather than write, they can also be tempted by the stimulating research projects they have encountered to set themselves unreal standards. It will be hard to sustain their commitment without a degree of adult input that will itself endanger the future of the project because it dilutes the child's sense of ownership. Half-finished, madcap schemes litter the lives of many creative children. The frustration, disappointment and confusion caused will eventually sap motivation as they recognize the pattern and lose faith in themselves.

GETTING THEM BACK ON TRACK

Taking each of the possible "causes" mentioned above in turn, do these suggestions contain something you can consider?

Inadequate Challenge

Find challenges for him in other areas, outside school. Some hobbies and interests can be followed at home if you have time and space to let him experiment. Introduce your child to someone who is knowledgeable about your child's special field of interest who might be able to spend time with him.

Local museums, libraries or other places of interest often run special days for children. Explore whether there are any special activities for very able children available locally, for example, Explorers Clubs organized by the National Association for Gifted Children, GIFT workshops or groups organized by Children with High Intelligence (CHI).

Being Put Down

Nurture your child's self-esteem and self-worth. A child who feels "hammered in" will have a greater need to be accepted at home. Accept him for who he is, not for what he can do—his special abilities—so that if he is teased for this talent, he has some self-esteem remaining.

Try to value him for his humor. Early humor is painful, but without those early attempts, no one will become skilled. Practice makes perfect.

Encourage relationships with other sympathetic adults. Feeling comfortable with a parent when the world outside seems so difficult can make a child quite dependent and untrusting of others.

Underperformance

Give him the space and freedom to work at his natural level at home, but try not to make too much fuss about what he achieves. He is doing it for himself, not for glory. Try to avoid showing the astonishment your child finds so tedious from others; let him feel normal. Let him keep ownership of this work.

Research ways in which your child can spend time with like-minded children, and even like-minded adults, with the same passions.

Frustration

A gifted child will become frustrated because his ideas run ahead of his ability to carry them out. Discuss more realistic targets, and then help him think through ways to achieve them. This will encourage stickability, develop planning skills and put the fast flow of ideas so typical of very able children to constructive use. Helping him to experience success and pride, not failure and frustration, will prevent him from never really fulfilling his promise—the "busted flush" syndrome.

Try not to take his project over. The safest approach is to ask, not assume, that our help will be welcomed. "Is there anything I can do that you would find helpful?" will give him the choice about how much support he accepts.

A NOTE OF CAUTION

To be happy in life and relationships, children need social skills that help them to fit in, but often gifted children don't fit. Parents of gifted children have the difficult task of finding a balance between allowing the child to be himself—perhaps insistent, impatient, sounding bossy or arrogant—and preparing him for the sometimes harsh world that finds such characteristics difficult to stomach.

It is a balance that some will not be very interested to achieve. Those who feed off their very bright child to fuel their own self-worth may need to encourage the talents that set their child clearly apart to "prove" and constantly reinforce his difference. The further danger is that he may become one-dimensional, and value himself exclusively through his talent. Pandering also to a parental need for status and to his need for parental approval, he can become almost a pastiche of himself as he acts out the role of the gifted child. Professor Joan Freeman, a writer and authority on gifted children, calls these youngsters "the career gifted." It is easy, then, for such children to slip into a permanent role as a "one-off" eccentric. Yet we have seen that personal success depends on much more than raw IQ. Employers increasingly demand team players, not loners and eccentrics. Personal relationships require compromise and empathy if they are to last and be fulfilling.

Gifted children, who start their lives with such a potential asset, need support to gain insight about their impact on the world. If they are to capitalize on their talents, they will need to become sensitive and adaptable while retaining the important bits of who they are.

DIAGRAM 21.1   Troubleshooter's Guide

	Signs of motivation difficulties	Possible reason	Possible action by parent
Stage One IDENTIFY THE TARGET	Unwilling to commit to a target Unable to decide what to aim at No aims or ambitions Inappropriate targets – too easy or too hard	Low self-esteem and belief, so assumes failure – future does not feel safe Poor sense of who he is Uncertain of what he wants or can do Personal or parental expectations too low/high	Make the future seem safe through a safer present Build his self-belief Find good role models for inspiration and example Help him to set more realistic targets
Stage Two ASSESS AND DEVELOP COMPETENCE	No interest in trying new things Thinks skills not worth improving because not good enough to start with	Low self-confidence. Feels generally incapable Fears change because uncertain of self Tendency to make or to be told about comparisons with others who are better	Encourage a variety of interests and talents Nurture child's self-esteem and confidence. Praise more, criticise, nag and punish less Show interest and pride in all his skills as they develop
Stage Three PLANNING THE ROUTE	Unwilling to think about creating a plan Plans tend to be impractical. Unrealistic expectations about what can be managed	Personal experiences have been unsettling Low trust in the ability to do anything well, and used to being directed Unwilling to take responsibility for effort made	Make home more predictable and secure. Provide routines and loving relationships Model planning skills – think ahead, make lists and break tasks down Make child responsible for his behavior Discuss cutting down television and computer games
Stage Four APPLICATION AND DETERMINATION	Gives up very easily when problems surface Seems to run out of steam Leaves everything to the last minute so quality affected	Finds it hard to problem-solve, evaluate and alter performance Unable to concentrate, easily bored, target too distant or parent competing Poor time management	Make it safe for him to make mistakes. Discuss what goes right or wrong, and why, together Offer incentives. Make it fun. Show interest, encouragement and commitment. Don't compete Encourage routines, agree priorities and time plans
Stage Five SUCCESS	Success never good enough. Devalues own achievements Gives up just before the finishing line Invests everything in success in one field only	Striving for acceptance through self-improvement and perfection Fears responsibility for keeping high standard. Avoids the final judgement for fear of failing Feels accepted for achievements, not self	Let him own the success, and celebrate it to prove it's good enough Accept him for who he is, not what he can do Help him with the last push. Reward stickability Value many talents

Bibliography

Adair, John. (1983) *Effective Leadership.* Pan, London.

Ames, Carole. (1992) Classrooms: Goals, Structures, and Student Motivation. *Journal of Educational Psychology* 84 (3):261–271.

Ball, Christopher. (1994) *Start Right: The Importance of Early Learning.* RSA, London.

Blanchard, Kenneth, and Spencer Johnson. (1981) *The One Minute Manager.* Collins, London.

Burningham, Sally. (1994) *Young People Under Stress.* Virago/Mind, London.

ChildLine. (1996) *Stressed Out: What Children Tell ChildLine About Exams and Work Pressure.* A ChildLine study.

City of Westminster. (1996) *Working with Very Able Children.*

Csikszentmihalyi, M., K. Rathunde, and S. Whalen. (1993) *Talented Teenagers: The Roots of Success and Failure.* Cambridge University Press, Cambridge.

Davy, Annie. (1995) *Playwork: Play and Care for Children 5–15.* Macmillan, London.

de Bono, Edward. (1974) *Children Solve Problems.* Harper & Row, New York.

Dunn, J. (1988) *The Beginnings of Social Understanding.* Basil Blackwell, Oxford.

Freeman, J. (1991) *Gifted Children Growing Up.* Cassel Educational Ltd., London.

Fulton, David. (1994) Discouraged Children: When Praise Does Not Help. *British Journal of Special Education* 214:166–168.

Gardner, H. (1983) *Frames of Mind: The Theory of Multiple Intelligences.* Basic Books, New York.

———. (1993) *The Unschooled Mind: How Children Think and How Schools Should Teach.* Fontana Press, London.

George, D. (1992) *The Challenge of the Able Child*. David Fulton, London.

Ginott, Haim. (1969) *Between Parent and Child*. Avon Books, New York.

Goleman, D. (1996) *Emotional Intelligence*. Bloomsbury, London.

Gough, Darren. (1996) *Darren Gough's Book for Young Cricketers*. Hodder and Stoughton, London.

Graham, Philip. (1995) *So Young, So Sad, So Listen*. Gaskell/West London Health Promotion Agency, London.

Greenhalgh, P. (1994) *Emotional Growth and Learning*. Routledge, London.

Haldane, J. M., and M. Taylor, eds. (1996) *Values in Education and Education in Values*. Falmer Press, London.

Hall, E., and C. Hall. (1988) *Human Relations in Education*. Routledge, London.

———. (1990) *Scripted Fantasy in the Classroom*. Routledge, London.

Hall, H., G. Roberts, and D. Treasure. (1994) Parental Goal Orientations and Beliefs About the Competitive Sports Experience of their Child. *Journal of Sports Psychology* 24 (7):631–645.

Hall, H. K., and A. W. Kerr. (1997) Motivational Antecedents of Precompetitive Anxiety in Youth Sport. *The Sports Psychologist* 1124:42.

Handy, C. (1983) *Understanding Organisations*. Penguin Books Ltd., London.

———. (1994) *The Empty Raincoat*. Arrow Business Books, London.

———. (1995) *Beyond Certainty*. Arrow Business Books, London.

———. (1997) *The Hungry Spirit*. Hutchinson, London.

Hanko, G. (1995) *Special Needs in Ordinary Classrooms: From Staff Support to Staff Development,* 3rd ed. David Fulton, London.

Hartley-Brewer, E. (1988) *Positive Parenting: Raising Children with Self-Esteem*. Vermilion, London.

———. (1996) *Cooperative Kids*. Hartley-Brewer Parenting Projects.

———. (1996) *School Matters, and So Do Parents!* Hartley-Brewer Parenting Projects.

Hattersley, Roy. (1983) *A Yorkshire Boyhood*. Oxford University Press, Oxford.

Health Education Authority. (1995) *Expectations for the Future: An Investigation into the Self Esteem of 13- and 14-Year-Old Girls and Boys.*

Holt, J. (1990) *How Children Fail.* Penguin Books, London.

House of Commons Health Committee. (1997) *Fourth Report, Child and Adolescent Mental Health Services: Report and Proceedings.* The Stationary Office, London.

Hunt, J. (1981) *Managing People at Work.* Pan Books, London.

Lewis, D. (1993) *Helping Your Anxious Child.* Cedar, London.

Linden, J. (1996) Growing *Up: From Eight Years to Young Adulthood.* National Children's Bureau.

Linden, J., and L. Linden. (1994) *Help Your Child Through School.* Hodder Headway, London.

Lindenfield, G. (1996) *Self-Motivation.* Thorsons, London.

McCormack, M. H. (1984) *What They Don't Teach You at the Harvard Business School.* Fontana/Collins, London.

National Commission on Education. (1993) *Learning to Succeed.* Heinemann, London.

National Council for Educational Technology. (1994) *IT Works: Learning Together with Computers.* NCET, London.

Nierenberg, G. I. (1975) *How to Give and Receive Advice.* Editorial Correspondents, New York.

———. (1981) *The Art of Negotiating.* Simon and Schuster, New York.

Noonan, E. (1989) *Counselling Young People.* Tavistock/Routledge, London.

Pipher, M. (1994) *Reviving Ophelia.* Ballantine Books, New York.

Pollard, A., with A. Filer. (1996) *The Social World of Children's Learning.* Cassell, London.

Russell, A., and R. Russell. (1996) *Information Technology for Parents.* Piccadilly Press, London.

Sylva, K. (1994) The Impact of Early Learning on Children's Later Development, Appendix C in *Start Right.* RSA, London.

Tizard, B., and M. Hughes. (1984) *Young Children Learning.* Fontana, London.

Vroom, V., and E. Deci, eds. (1983) *Management and Motivation.* Penguin, London.

Young Minds. (1996) *Mental Health in Your School: A Guide for Teachers and Others Working in Schools.* Jessica Kingsley Publishers, London.

Acknowledgments

Writing this book has been one of the hardest things I have ever done, testing my own motivation on occasions. Putting my theory into practice, I sought honest feedback from a number of friends and colleagues as the book took shape, to spur me on. I would like to thank Gillian Pugh, Gerda Hanko, Titus Alexander, Dominic Regan and John Coleman, who had the difficult job of commenting on particular chapters or sections without the benefit of seeing them in the context of the completed book, as well as Victoria Hipps and Sarah Sutton for their editorial guidance. Their comments, guidance and suggestions for further reading were invaluable.

Particular thanks are due, first, to Charles and Elizabeth Handy for agreeing to my request to meet to discuss motivation within organizations and families, and, second, to Dr. Howard Hall, Principal Lecturer in Sports Psychology at De Montfort University, Bedford, who was very generous with his time explaining his work and that of other researchers in his field. I have not been able to include all that Dr. Hall covered, so any omissions are my responsibility.

I will remain eternally grateful to my family. I thank my two children, Stephen and Georgia, for tolerating my preoccupation, for their love and for their sensible reactions and straight talking, which have taught me so much, and my step-daughter, Julia, whose unquenchable wit and vitality lifts all our spirits.

Finally, I would like to say a warm thank you to all those friends who agreed to let me use their stories.

Author's Note

Throughout the text the child is referred to as "he," except when a specific child is being referred to; however, all the content of this book applies equally to boys and girls.

The examples given on page 78 appeared first in *The Independent* and are reprinted with their kind permission.

Other books in this series available from Da Capo Press by Elizabeth Hartley-Brewer

Raising Happy Kids
ISBN: 0–306–81316–5

Raising Confident Boys
ISBN: 1–55561–320–9

Raising Confident Girls
ISBN: 1–55561–321–7